HISTORIC ARCHAEOLOGY AT THE TUCSON COMMUNITY CENTER

By James E. Ayres

Prepared for

The Tucson Development Corporation

Cultural Resource Management Division
Arizona State Museum
The University of Arizona

1990

Archaeological Series 181

TABLE OF CONTENTS

LIST OF TABLES

LIST OF FIGURES

Chapter 1

INTRODUCTION

The archaeology for the Tucson Convention Center Expansion Project, sponsored by the Tucson Local Development Corporation (TLDC), was performed by archaeologists from the Cultural Resource Management Division (CRMD) of the Arizona State Museum (ASM). Project fieldwork was carried-out in two stages, testing and mitigation, between mid-March and mid-May, 1988. Laboratory work, artifact identification and analysis, historical research, and report preparation, followed the fieldwork phase over the subsequent two years. The project was the first of an archaeological nature undertaken by the TLDC, a private non-profit corporation created by the City of Tucson in 1979. This organization provides long-term financing for small business expansion in the Tucson Metro area and eastern Pima County.

Project History

The Tucson Convention Center Expansion Project began in March 1988 when the TLDC circulated a competitive solicitation for consultant services to evaluate the archaeological potential within the area of the proposed project. The consulting services included providing assistance in planning for the archaeological requirements the TLDC might confront, and in formulating mitigation strategies.

The CRMD responded to the RFP, and on April 5, 1988, was awarded the contract and given notice to proceed. The first deliverable was an overview report assessing the archaeological potential of the project area. A study of the Sanborn Fire Insurance maps clearly indicated the high potential for significant historic remains in all the lots involved. Further, the project area had seen no previous archaeological excavations. Because of the likelihood that significant historical remains existed, the overview report included recommendations for an archaeological testing program (Ayres 1988a).

The testing proposal was approved by the TLDC in mid-April and fieldwork commenced immediately thereafter. Testing was conducted from April 18-26, 1988. On April 28, 1988, a preliminary report of the testing results was submitted to the TLDC (Ayres 1988b). The report recommended measures to mitigate the impacts of Convention Center construction to a number of the historically significant trash deposits found during testing.

The archaeological testing phase was promptly followed by a mitigation phase that was performed over a two week period from May 2-13, 1988. Overall, the Convention Center Expansion Project archaeological studies were greatly shaped by time and money constraints. Very little lead time was provided between submission of proposals for the various phases of work and notices to proceed, and minimal time was allowed to complete each phase. For the most part, this was a project where the archaeological input came much later in the planning and construction sequence than is desirable. Construction activity was on-going throughout the mitigation phase.

In addition, late in the process, due to various construction project cost overruns, a nearly 50% reduction in the original proposed budget for artifact analysis and report preparation was made. This meant that the final analysis and report would be less substantial than we had planned. For example, the analysis of the faunal remains, which was key to addressing the main research question related to food behavior, was only partially achieved.

Throughout the process, the question was raised as to whether or not the TLDC, as a private nonprofit corporation, was legally required to be concerned with the historic archaeological remains. To this end the requirements of the "Tucson Cultural Resource Protection Resolution" (No. 12443) dated October 3, 1983, were brought to bear. To its credit, the TLDC through its Project Director Gary Molenda, stretched its already tight project budget to sponsor these studies of Tucson's important historic remains and agreed to provide funding for the preparation of the overview, for testing and mitigation, and for subsequent artifact and data analysis and report preparation. This was indeed a notable public service.

The Project Area

The project area where archaeological testing and mitigation were recommended and performed includes lots 6, 7, and 17 in historic Block 228 and lot 12 in Historic Block 221, in downtown Tucson, Arizona (Fig. 1.1). It is situated in the center of the NW 1/4 of Section 23, in T14S, R13E.

The configuration of these lots, essentially unchanged from the early 1870s to the late 1960s, was dramatically altered when the Tucson Convention Center, part of Tucson's Urban Renewal effort, was constructed between 1969 and 1971. Prior to Urban Renewal, the lots in Block 228 were typically of residential use, while the Block 221 lots were primarily of commercial use or vacant.

Formerly Lot 12 of Block 221 was bounded on the east by Main Street. Block 228 was bounded by Main Street on the west, Meyer Street on the east, McCormick Street on the north and Simpson Street on the south. This exceptionally large block was cut in half when Cushing Street was put through it about 1968 Cushing Street now forms the southern boundary of the Convention Center property and of the project area.

With Convention Center construction between 1969 and 1971, the existing historic street pattern was radically altered. Block 221 and lots 6, 7, and 17 of Block 228 became parts of Convention Center parking lots.

The Testing Program

Backhoe testing of the affected parts of Block 228 and Block 221 was performed during the period April 18-26, 1988 (Ayres 1988b). CRMD Archaeologists Thomas Euler and Ronald Gardiner were responsible for documenting the text excavations and results. Some field time was lost during the testing phase due to rain and because the project area had not been cleared of rubble and portions of the parking lot asphalt. As a result of the latter, we were unable to perform testing in about one-quarter of the area designated for it. This area was also the location of the asphalt that had been removed in pieces, and piled from the rest of the property.

The first area tested was the approximately 3200 sq. ft. parking lot on the south side of the Convention Center Arena. Of the 18 backhoe trenches placed there, 16 were oriented north-south across the lot and two on the southern edge of the lot were oriented east-west. The trenches were spaced at 10-foot intervals and varied from about 100 ft. to 150 ft. in length depending on the space available. The trenches were excavated to a maximum depth of 4 ft., or to sterile caliche, whichever came first. On the north end of the lot, the caliche was 4 ft. or more below the present ground surface. On the south side, it was consistently less than 1 ft. below surface. A site datum was established on the south side of the area being tested.

Testing Methods

Three north-south trenches, approximately 30 ft. long, were placed 10 ft. apart and were excavated in the 50 ft. by 60 ft. affected area in Block 221 at the northwest corner of the former intersection of Main Avenue and Cushing Street. No significant historic remains were encountered at this location, and no further archaeological effort was recommended for this area.

During testing the trenches, trash deposits, and building footings and foundations were mapped and photographed. Profile drawings were made of all the major trash deposits. Trenches were subsequently backfilled except those containing historic remains thought likely to have the potential to yield information important to the history of Tucson.

Testing Results

Disturbance of the project area as a result of the original 1969 to 1971 construction of the Convention Center was generally minimal. Building demolition disturbed the historic ground surface, and subsequent development of lots 6, 7, and 17 as a parking lot required the placing of several inches of caliche excavated from the Convention Center site on top of it. More caliche was placed on the southern end of the area than on the north. A thin layer of gravel and blacktop paving was then placed over the caliche. Thus, as a result of the previous construction activities, we were unable to ascertain the location of the original ground surface.

Throughout all the lots a discontinuous sheet trash deposit of varying thickness lay under the caliche layer. In many cases this deposit was lying over the features. At the junction of the caliche layer and the sheet trash recent artifacts, such as pieces of plastic and beer bottles, were found mixed with historic period artifacts. At the conclusion of the testing only two general areas within the parking lot were found to contain intact deposits of historic artifacts (Fig. 1.2). These were believed to be significant deposits.

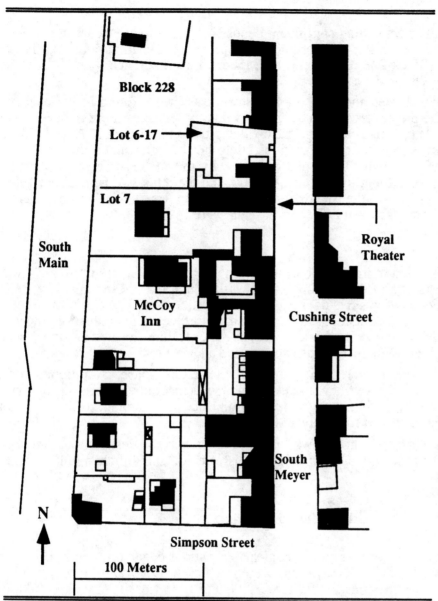

Figure 1.1
Project Location

Area 1

One of the two areas containing significant deposits referred to as Area 1 in the field, was believed to have been within the backyard of the property designated variously as 313 or 315 South Main Street (Block 228, Lot 7) on the Sanborn Fire Insurance maps.   Specific feature identifications for this area are shown in Chapter 1.

A number of small lenses and pockets of historic trash were found in the backhoe trenches in this part of the project area. After careful evaluation, most of these trenches were profiled and backfilled. Three relatively large trash-filled pits, were located. in Area 1. Their depths (at least four feet) and exact configurations could not be determined during testing without irreparably damaging them. These pits were thought to be filled-in wells or latrines. One pit appeared to date from approximately 1890-1900, and the other two from about 1900-1915. Also found in this area was the foundation remains of the Royal Theater, consistently misidentified on the Sanborn Maps as the "Teatro Carmen".

Area 2

A second concentration of historic deposits, given the field designation "Area 2," was located in the northeast portion of the parking lot. It was thought that these remains were in what was once the backyards of lots 6 and 17 of Block 228. Like Area 1, Area 2 contained a number of small lenses and pits containing historic trash. After a careful evaluation, most of these were profiled and the trenches were backfilled. The major features located in Area 2 were a large, approximately 25 feet in diameter, trash deposit and a latrine pit.

In all, 11 feature numbers were assigned during the testing phase. Additional work, specifically archaelogical data recovery through excavation, was recommended for ten of these. Feature 3, a thin, extensive layer of sheet trash identified in Lot 7, was thought to be redundant and was therefore not recommended for excavation.

For the purposes of subsequent fieldwork and for this report the designations "Area 1" and "Area 2" were dropped; and the appropriate historic lot and block numbers were substituted.

Mitigation of Impacts

Mitigation efforts in the form of archaeological excavations began on May 2, 1988 and were concluded on May 13, 1988.   Excavations were initiated in Lot 7 and by May 5 work progressed in all the lots simultaneously. Features 2, 9, and 10 in Lot 6; features 1 and 8 in Lot 17; and features 4-7 and 11 in the western half of Lot 7 had been identified during the testing phase and were subsequently excavated.

Features 1 and 8, although of relatively minor importance, were the only features discovered in Lot 17 and were excavated primarily to provide a sample of material from that lot. During the course of excavating Feature 11, minor features 12 and 13 were located and excavated. The excavation of the intriguing and puzzling circular pits in Lot 7, exemplified by features 4 and 5, led to the stripping of an area to the south in search of others. This effort resulted in the discovery of one additional circular pit, Feature 17, and two small pits, features 14 and 16. Feature 15, one of the circular pits, was found during excavation of Feature 11. Feature 3 which was found during testing, and Feature 14 were not excavated, primarily because of time considerations. Feature 16 was not excavated because it appeared to be of recent origin. Features 6 and 15 were not completely excavated because of their depths. The bottom of Feature 15 was located by backhoe and much of its lower fill was removed without screening. The bottom of Feature 6 was not located. Because of its size, Feature 2 was only sampled.

Research Goals

The research goals of the Tucson Convention Center archaeological project were presented in a report submitted to the TLDC in May 1988 (Ayres 1988c).

One of the initial project research tasks at the conclusion of the excavations was to establish locations of all features within their appropriate historic lot boundaries. Most useful in this regard were the remains of the *Teatro Carmen* foundation. This foundation was encountered in several of the backhoe trenches (trenches 1, 16, 2, 15, 3, 14, 4, and 5) during the testing phase. Its southwest corner was found near the surface between trenches 5 and 12. This corner provided an accurate reference point from which to identify other features shown on the Sanborn and other maps (Fig. 1.3). Some inconsistencies were present, however. One of the privies in the northeastern study area

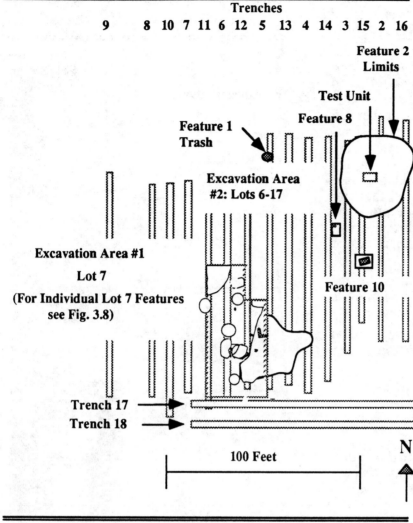

Figure 1.2

Excavation Areas and Backhoe Trenches

is recorded within the boundaries of Lot 17, as shown here, in the excavation maps, while it may be associated with Lot 6 on theSanborn map.   The author has chosen to discuss the feature in the location shown on the Sanborn map, but it should be noted that this is inconsistent with excavation map evidence.

Next, the preparation of a detailed history of the three project area lots, using the standard historical sources available for Tucson, was necessary. The sources and procedures for this are discussed below.

Finally, it was necessary to date artifacts from each feature as accurately as possible. Having features accurately dated and the lot histories established, it was expected that assignment of a specific feature and its artifacts to a specific property owner or lot resident would be possible.

Completing these three basic research tasks provided the background information necessary to assess the artifacts and other data in terms of the research questions, and to integrate the archaeological with the historical data.

The artifacts from this site were of particular interest and importance because they provided a unique insight into the life styles and behavior of some of the average, ordinary inhabitants of historic Tucson. These individuals are poorly represented, if at all, in the traditional histories of Tucson and Arizona.

It originally was intended that project research would focus on food, dietary, and consumer behavior, and food preparation activities as reflected through artifacts and faunal remains. It was thought that assemblages generated by turn-of-the-century Mexican residents would be noticeably different from assemblages generated by Anglos residents. If the trash from both groups was present, it was intended that our research would attempt to explore the differences and establish whether or not assemblages became increasingly similar over time.

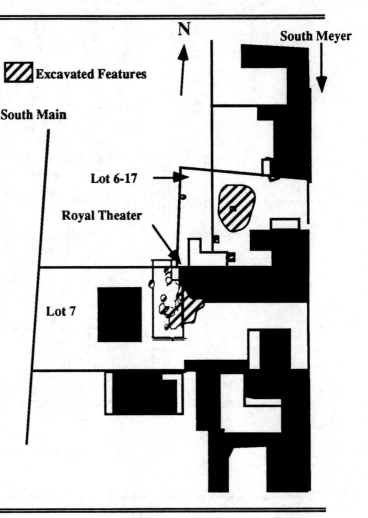

Figure 1.3

Excavated Features Superimposed on Sanborn Map Data

These general statements of the research goals can be presented in more specific terms. Examples of these are:

1. What was the variety of food types present and how did they vary through time?

2. Large quantities of butchered bone were recovered, does the butchering reflect Mexican or Anglo techniques, or both?

3. Do the food related artifacts and the faunal remains indicate that the inhabitants of these lots enjoyed a balanced diet?

4. Did wild game supplement the diet?

5. Was there a reliance on national and international sources for food, rather than on local sources?

6. Is there evidence for increased reliance on eastern manufactured goods over those produced locally or regionally?

7. Specifically, what were the sources of food products for Tucson?

8. What was the role of the Papago and Mexican made ceramics in the households being studied?

9. Was the use of Papago and Mexican made ceramics confined to Mexican households?

10. Do the artifacts reflect a change in the use of the various lots over time?

The lack of funding to pursue the complete analysis of the faunal remains inhibited our ability to address these research questions as fully as intended.

Field and Laboratory Methods

Standard and traditional ASM field procedures and forms were used throughout the testing and mitigation phases of the project. Each artifact bag was assigned its own number and was recorded on a bag number list. Each feature was recorded, logged on a feature description list, photographed, profiled, and drawn in plan view. A general descriptive feature form was filled-out for each feature, along with one for each excavation stratum and level, and general field notes were maintained in a project field journal. A crew of six individuals was employed to carry out the mitigation effort.

Excavation of most of the features began by having the backhoe remove the layer of redeposited caliche that had been spread over the site during previous parking lot construction. For the most part, the caliche was removed over horizontal areas only slightly larger than the assumed extent of individual features in the case of vertical features such as wells or latrines, or to the horizontal extent of arbitrarily chosen excavation units established over trash deposits, such as features 2 and 11. From this point, excavation was accomplished by hand. In the deposits often overlying the tops of features, excavation followed natural stratagraphic units whenever possible. The same strategy was applied to Feature 2, a large trash deposit. Fill in the confined spaces of wells and privies was generally removed in 2 ft. levels. Variations in these general practices are discussed under individual feature descriptions below. All excavated fill was screened through 1/4 in. mesh hardware cloth, with the exception of Feature 1, the lower part of Feature 15, and the sheet trash over deep features. Finally, a site map was prepared using a plane table and alidade. At the request of the construction contractor's field supervisor, no backfilling was done at the conclusion of the project.

When removed to the laboratory, the sequentially numbered artifact bags were emptied and the artifacts were cleaned and rebagged. Few of the artifacts required special handling or treatment while being cleaned. The metal artifacts and the faunal remains were dry brushed; the rest were washed. During the cleaning process, the fauna was separated and boxed together in readiness for the faunal analysis.

A few metal artifacts, including cartridge cases and some clothing fasteners, received special cleaning. Many of these possess maker's marks, patent dates, brand names, caliber size, and other information useful in determining their dates and functions. To reduce the corrosion and to reveal information stamped on them, they were soaked in vinegar and brushed periodically until clean enough to be legible. Subsequently, all were washed in water to neutralize the acid.

Artifact identification and analysis were performed using level-by-level associations for each feature. The artifacts were sorted by material (glass, ceramic, metal, other), then by function within each material class. The classification system used was essentially identical to that presented by Hull-Walski and Ayres (1989).

Twelve functional categories were utilized. Most are self-explanatory, but two need further explanation. The "miscellaneous" category includes artifacts with identifiable forms but with unknown functions. Artifacts in the "unidentified" category are those for which neither the form nor the function is known.

During the analysis, two different artifact counts were made. First, the total number of whole and fragmentary pieces from each provenience was determined. Then the minimum number of individual artifacts represented by the pieces was estimated. Both figures are used throughout the feature description section below although "minimum number of objects" provides a more realistic view of the number of actual artifacts present. Where parts of the same artifact are found in two levels one artifact might unintentionally be counted as two artifacts.

Historical Research

Subsequent to mitigation, a more detailed history than had been done for the overview was completed for the three lots. Four major sources of information were utilized to determine who owned and who occupied these lots through time, their ethnic affiliation, the changes in use of the block through time, and other relevant material. These were: city directories, to discover the actual occupants of the houses on the three lots; the various property ownership records to find who owned the three lots through time; the U.S. Decennial Census schedules, to determine family size, ages, whether homes were owned or rented, and other personal information; and the Sanborn Fire Insurance maps, for information about the architectural character of Block 228. The census schedules were of use only for the years 1900 and 1910.

Unfortunately not all the occupants of the dwellings on lots 6, 7, and 17 were listed in the city directories. As a result, the list of occupants is very incomplete. Establishing the names of property owners through time was easier, but owners often did not occupy the dwellings they owned on Block 228.

Report Content

The features and artifacts found in lots 6, 7, and 17, of Block 228, are described below. Descriptions of artifacts are purposefully kept to a minimum, but some descriptive information is included to help the reader understand the nature of the cultural remains from the various features and to allow evaluation of interpretations made from them. Where quantities are large enough, artifacts are grouped by functional categories and provenience on a series of tables for each feature. Where few artifacts for a given function exist, for marked and dated artifacts, for decorated ceramics, and for "special" artifacts such as those reflecting ethnicity or reflecting use by women and children, discussion in the text is necessary.

For convenience, all of the Mexican and Papago made ceramics are listed in the tables for food preparation and consumption. These ceramics are assumed to have been used directly and indirectly for cooking, serving, and storing food. No Papago forms were identified that could be attributed to a function other than food preparation and consumption .

For the same reason all faunal remains are listed under the food function; with few exceptions all relate to that category. The faunal remains were completely identified only for features 7 and 10, and partially for Feature 5. Faunal remains were recovered from every feature but a sample consisting of 3 of 15 boxes (20 percent) was analyzed. The faunal counts were kept separate from other artifact totals.

In this report, a number of commonly found artifacts are assigned arbitrary dates that more or less reflect reality. These are sun-colored glass (SCA), 1880 to 1919; turned pink glass, 1919 to the 1940s; square cut nails, 1860 to 1900; and wire nails, 1890 to the present. The turned pink glass, as well as straw colored glass, appears to result from the use of selenium as a decolorizer in the glass batch. Selenium replaced manganese as a decolorizer sometime about 1919. Whether a piece of glass turns pink or straw colored seems to be dependent on the amount of selenium used. Kendrick (1963: 45) and Giarde (1980: 164-165) assign a date of 1914 to 1930 to straw or honey colored glass. Giarde states that pink glass dates post-1910. A beginning date of 1914 for both pink and straw colored glass may accurately reflect the initial use of selenium by some glass companies, but the 1930 end date is incorrect because examples that date to the early 1940s are known. The 1919 date used in this report may not be early enough.

Turned pink glass has not been reported in an archaeological context, except in the case of the Plan 6 Project (Hull-Walski and Ayres 1989), probably because it occurs relatively late in time and because it may be misidentified by the casual observers as SCA glass to which it appears similar.

The dates derived from artifacts are presented on a table for each feature. Descriptions and dates of artifacts are also included in the text. When an end date is unknown, or if the end date is essentially the present, an arbitrary end date of 1950 is used as a convenient convention.

Dates for the various studied artifacts vary considerably in their degree of reliability. Some are very firm and others are barely adequate estimates; taken together, all are useful in determining the dates of deposition of the trash in each feature.

Acknowledgements

An effort the size of the Tucson Convention Center Archaeological Project requires the direct or indirect participation of many individuals to bring it to a successful conclusion. Lynn S. Teague and Susan A. Brew, Principal Investigator and Project Director respectively, provided the overall direction for the project and assumed all of the administrative responsibilities and editorial chores. As Project Director, Brew's enthusiasm and concern for the TCC historic resources made my work easier throughout, and her natural effervescence provided a mainstay to me during the report preparation period.

The co-field supervisors for both the testing and mitigation field work were Ronald Gardiner and Thomas Euler. Gardiner and Euler served as the filed crew during the testing. Field crew members during the data recovery phase were Claudine Chisholm, Ed Wright, Steven Troncone, Jon Goodfellow, and Reiner Vanderpot. All served the project admirably.

Later Steve Troncone and Jon Goodfellow assumed responsibility for cleaning the artifacts and supervising the laboratory crew members provided by Project Origins staff. The latter washed artifacts, labeled them, and prepared the faunal remains for analysis.

Additionally, the backhoe was operated by Bob Foote and Dan Arnet from Bob Foote Excavating, Jennifer Strand performed the faunal analysis, and Sharon Urban provided the identification of the shell. Sue Ruiz typed the report and Lynn Teague and Ann D'Onofrio provided the expertise to create the numerous tables from my rough drafts.

CHAPTER 2

HISTORY

In this chapter an historic overview of Block 228 is presented. The general character of the block, its uses or functions over time, and the changes in its appearance are described. This overview is followed by a discussion of the specific nature of the three lots in which archaeological excavations were performed, of the changes through time in the use of the lots, of their architecture, and of the history of ownership and residency.

Block 228

Block 228 was exceptionally large by Tucson standards, in fact it was the size of two blocks. It was located between Meyer and Main streets on the east and west and by Mc Cormick and Simpson on the north and south . The year the block was first laid out and occupied was not determined, but it must have been in 1872 when the Village of Tucson was officially created. Beginning in 1872, the Village of Tucson began selling lots on Block 228. The block is shown on Foreman's 1872 map of Tucson; the area is not included on the Ferguson map of 1862.

Shortly before 1919 the block was renumbered as two blocks: 939 on the north and 979 on the south. About 1968 the block was physically divided when Cushing Street was extended westward through it.

It must be noted that although historic sites archaeologists necessarily rely on Sanborn Map data to assess important aspects of historic use of an area such as determining numbers of residences and determining the functions of buildings, there are problems inherent with their use. For example, most residences are identified by "D" of "Dwg", but many that were not marked, especially in the rear of lots, were undoubtedly also used as residences. Of these, only those buildings having street numbers, always with a fraction (for example, 424 1/2), were counted as dwellings. Also, because many residences were a part of Sonoran row houses, that is a series of contiguous buildings located at the edge of the street, it was difficult to accurately determine the actual number of separate residences within each row. In these cases, the counts were based on the street numbers, with each number counted as one residence.

Also, these Sanborn maps are not always accurate in their labeling of building use or function. A known example of this problem in Block 228 was for the building or row house on the northwest corner. The maps consistently label this complex as residences, but at least part of it had use for several years as U.S. Government offices. Because the complete period of its use as offices was not researched, the complex is considered as residences for the purposes of this study.

A review of 10 Sanborn map sets of Tucson dating from 1883 to 1930 reveals that over time Block 228 was remarkably stable in its mix of dwellings and businesses, in the types of buildings present, and in the types of businesses located there. Tables 2.1 and 2.2 summarize the Sanborn map information on residential and business use for the 47 year period studied.

Block 228 can be characterized as one experiencing gradual infilling of the vacant space fronting the streets and to some degree in the interior of lots. The majority of this activity took place on Meyer Street. Along with this, as the number of residences steadily increased, so did the population. There were no sudden or dramatic shifts in population or in the number of buildings present anytime between 1883 and 1919. The year 1919 saw the peak in the number of residences on the block, and thus in population. By 1930, the number of residences and by extension the population, may have declined by as much as 32 percent. A very gradual decline or near stability in numbers of block occupants occurred from about 1930 to 1968 at which time the north half of the block was demolished to accommodate construction of the Convention Center.

Dwelling Type	Sanborn Map Year									
	1883	1886	1889	1896	1901	1904	1909	1914	1919	1930
Row House Block	4	4	4	4	4	4	4	4	4	4
Duplex	1	1	1	1	1	1	1	1	1	
Single	8	8	8	9	15	15	17	18	12	8
Dwellings in Backyards	4	6	6	5	8	8	8	8	10	5
Buildings identified as "rooms"									2	2
Buildings identified as "tenements"					1	1	1	1	2	2
All buildings identified as "dwellings"	25	31	31	24	35	37	40	39	48	33
Vacant	3	2	2	1						

Table 2.1
Dwelling Types on Block 228

For the sake of illustration, and if we assume an average household size of five individuals, the 1883 population of Block 228 might have been about 125 people based on the number of dwellings estimated from the Sanborn map. A decline occurred in 1896 but this may be more apparent than real; at any rate it cannot be explained without further research. Based on our assumptions, a gradual population increase occurred over time until about 1919 when the population reached approximately 240 individuals. By 1930 the block had decreased in population to about 165 people, or by 32 percent. These figures are based on the number of dwellings and do not include buildings labeled as "tenements" or "rooms".

Throughout its history, Block 228 contained a mix of residences and businesses, but primarily it was part of a larger residential neighborhood. The Meyer Street side of the block and the northwest corner with its adobe row houses, was more typical of urban Tucson before 1900 than was the Main Street side. The Main Street part of the block reflected a totally different pattern, consisting of large lots, single family residences set back from the edge of the street, larger houses, and the only brick houses on the block. There were two all brick houses and one with a brick facing located along Main Street. These factors, plus the more open, less crowded aspect of the west side of the block, all suggest more affluent residents. The Main Street pattern reflects a more Anglo type of residency as opposed to the Meyer Street side which was typically Sonoran in character.

The major concentration of buildings and people was always on the Meyer Street part of the block and all of the businesses were on Meyer Street up to about 1919. Around 1919 one of the residences on Main Street was listed as "tenements" and the 1930 map shows the buildings in the southwest corner of the block as a store. It also shows a bottling works on Simpson Street.

Sheridan (1986: 81, 123) illustrates the differences between the two sides of Block 228 on maps showing the percent of the Mexican population there. The data on these maps is of necessity overgeneralized. The Meyer Street side of the block had a 75 to 100 percent Mexican occupation in 1881 and the Main Street side was 25 to 49 percent Mexican occupied.

The latter percentage figures suggest that the Main Street side was 50 to 74 percent Anglo. In 1897 the Meyer Street side at its northeast corner, at its southeast corner, and along Simpson Street, were still 75 to 100 percent Mexican occupied. The center half had been diluted to only 50 to 74 percent Mexican. At the same time, at the northwest and southwest corners of Main Street, the figure was 25 to 49 percent Mexican, or the same as in 1881. The population along the rest of Main Street was 50 to 74 percent Mexican, which represented an increase in the number of Mexicans living there.

Business Type	Sanborn Map Year:									
	1883	1886	1889	1896	1901	1904	1909	1914	1919	1930
Food, Staples & Supplies										
Meat/Butcher	1	2	2	1						
Bread Store	1		1							
Bakery	"Vacant"			1	1	1		1		1
General Msde/										
General Store	1	1	1							
Chinese Store					1	1	1	1	1	1
Bottling Works										1
Personal Services										
Chinese Washhouse	1									
Cobbler			1	2						
Barber							1			
Leisure & Recreation										
Saloon					1	1	1	1		
Theater									2	1
Other										
"Store"				2	1	1	2	1	4	10
Unidentified		1	1							
Garage		1	1							1
Hog Warehouse									1	1
TOTALS	4	4	6	9	5	5	6	5	8	16

Table 2.2

Businesses on Block 228

Except for the meat or butcher shop, cobbler, theater, and "stores", only one business of a type was present on the block in the years the Sanborn maps were prepared. As Table 2.2 indicates, there were two butcher shops in 1886 and in 1889, two cobblers and two "stores" in 1896, two stores in 1909, two theaters and four "stores" in 1919, and 10 "stores" in 1930.

The generically labeled "stores" may easily have been selling dissimilar goods or services. The Chinese store, the grocery stores, and the general merchandise or general stores, may all have been selling groceries and other similar products.

There were a number of buildings labeled "storage" on the Sanborn maps over the years. This designation describes the use of the buildings and does not mean that they were businesses. Buildings labeled on the Sanborn maps as having a business function may also have served in part as dwellings for the proprietors.

Continuity of businesses on Block 228 was limited, but there were a few exceptions. The maps show a saloon at the northeast corner of the block from about 1901 to 1914. From 1896 to about 1919 a business was labeled first as "D&S", which is unidentified, then as a grocery, and finally by 1919 as a "store". It was located near the southeast corner of the block on Meyer Street. A general merchandise store was at one location from 1883 to 1896. Between 1896 and 1901 it became a Chinese general store and during 1914 the building was demolished to erect a brick theater building, the *Teatro Carmen*, in 1915. This theater survived as such until about 1920, continued as a dance hall, movie house, and served other purposes until 1926 when it was turned into a garage (Sheridan 1986: 200-202). The other theater on the block, the Royal, located on the east end of Lot 7, was build about 1918 and survived as a movie theater until 1935 (Tucson Directory Co. 1918; Arizona Directory Co. 1935). The Sanborn maps consistently reversed the locations of the two theaters from those given in the city directories which are most likely correct.

Building materials used in Block 228 were predominantly adobe and wood frame, with adobe the preferred material. Wood frame was most frequently used for small outbuildings, porches, and the like. There were no stone buildings; the only stone on the block was in the outdoor ovens. Brick buildings were added to the block slowly beginning about 1901 when the northeast corner adobes were replaced by a brick saloon. A house in the middle of the Main Street side of the block was faced with brick at the same time. One of the two brick theaters was added in 1915 and the other in 1918. By 1930 there were six all brick buildings on Block 228 and three partial brick buildings. There were two all brick houses and the house faced with brick on Main Street and a bottling works building made of brick on Simpson Street. The remaining brick buildings were all related to businesses located on Meyer Street.

On Block 228 brick was principally used for construction of business buildings. The only residential brick buildings were single family homes constructed on Main Street. One interesting characteristic of this block was the appearance of "tenements" beginning about 1901. These were undoubtedly inexpensive apartments rather than slums as the word often implies today. One was found in mid block on Meyer Street beginning about 1901 and one on Main Street began about 1919. "Furnished rooms" or simply "rooms" were two in number, both on Meyer Street, one the house on Lot 6 from about 1919, and the other, part of the tenement complex, from about 1914.

Chinese were present on the block. They were first represented on the Sanborn maps as proprietors of a washhouse in 1883 and as store keepers from about 1901 to at least 1930.

Finally, a number of wells, privies, and ovens are represented on the Sanborn maps (Table 2.3). The numbers of these are approximate, especially for the privies. Not all were labeled as such, nor were all that were present shown on the maps. The number of wells, four in 1883, had declined to one in 1896, the last year a well was shown on the maps.

Ovens were plotted from 1883 to 1914. All were built of stone, were domed, were round in plan, and were in backyards. One was in the northeast corner of the block, one was in the center, and one was in the southeast corner. It is interesting to note that all were on the Meyer Street side of the block.

					Sanborn Map Year					
Outdoor Feature	1883	1886	1889	1896	1901	1904	1909	1914	1919	1930
Well		4	4	1	1					
Privy		6	7	7	9	2	2	4	5	2
Oven		3	3*	3	3	2*	2*	2*	2*	
	* one not in use									

Table 2.3
Wells, Privies and Ovens

In summary, it can be said that the residents of Block 228 lived in a relatively stable neighborhood in a familiar and basically unchanging urban environment. They had easy access to groceries, other supplies, services, and leisure and recreational activities on the block.

Lot 6: Building History

Lot 6 of Block 228 was designated as such by 1872 when the town was originally laid out. The rhomboid-shaped lot was a maximum of 74 ft. wide north-south on its west end, 69 ft. wide at its east end, 81 ft. long east-west on its south side, and 79 ft. long on its north side.

The one story adobe house on Lot 6 which was designated 424 South Meyer Street, was first shown on the 1883 Sanborn map. How much earlier it was is unknown, but it may have been constructed around 1872. It was about 20 ft. east-west and 35 ft north-south in size. A frame shed extended along the entire west side. Also, a small frame building approximately 10 ft by 20 ft in size was located in the center of the lot against the west lot boundary line. This building was identified as 424 1/2 South Meyer Street on the 1883 map.

By 1886 the frame shed on the rear of the house had been removed and replaced with an adobe addition. Wood frame porches were also added on the north and west sides of the building. The house in 1886 was square in plan measuring about 35 ft. on a side. The small shed in the rear of the lot had been removed and apparently replaced by a larger building in what was later designated Lot 17.

The Sanborn maps for 1886, 1889, and 1896 indicate that no changes were made to the house during those years. Sometime between 1896 and 1901 a small, approximately 15 ft. square, adobe addition was made on the west side, thus reducing the size of the west porch that ran the length of the house. From about 1901 to sometime before 1919, the house was designated 304 south Meyer Street, and by 1919 it was known as 300 South Meyer.

Sometime between 1914 and 1919 Sanborn maps indicate that the house ceased being a "dwelling" and became "furnished rooms", a status it maintained until sometime between 1930 and 1942 when it reverted to a dwelling. It served in this capacity until it was destroyed by urban renewal in 1968. At that time the house had been in existence for at least 85 years.

Other than the small shed at the rear of the lot in 1883, only two other outbuildings were located in Lot 6 on the Sanborn maps. One was a privy placed against the south lot line between the house in Lot 6 and that in Lot 17. This privy was illustrated only on the 1896 Sanborn maps, it was designated Feature 10 during excavations in this lot in 1988. The 1919 map shows a small frame building on Meyer Street north of the house; its purpose is unknown.

Lot 17: Building History

This lot was originally part of Lot 1, Block 228, but by 1896 the Sanborn map indicates that a new lot was created on the west side of Lot 6. The rhomboid-shaped lot was about 50 ft. east-west and 80 ft. north-south in extent. The lot was narrower on the north end than on the south.

The first property transaction involving the lot occurred in 1902 when it was included in a sale of Lot 6. In fact, throughout their history, the two lots were never separated as the result of a sale.

The small, one story wood frame building on the lot was about 12 ft. north-south and 50 ft. east-west in size. This house was first shown in the 1886 Sanborn map indicating its construction sometime between 1883 and 1886. The building thus predated the division of Lot 1 into lots 1 and 17 by at least 10 years. From 1886 to 1896 the house was illustrated on the

Sanborn maps as one long building. From 1901 to 1919 it was shown as having two parts, possibly representing two apartments, although it only had one street number assignment to it. According to the maps, between 1914 and 1919 a small addition was made on the north side of the building at its west end.

Sometime between 1919 and 1922 the building on Lot 17 was demolished. The lot was never built upon afterwards.

From at least 1886 to about 1901 the building was designated 424 1/2 South Meyer Street. From about 1901 to sometime before 1919 it was known as 304 1/2 and by 1919 it was 300 1/2 South Meyer Street. The designation of this building as "one-half" indicates its role as an extension of the house in Lot 6 despite the fact that over half of its life it was situated on its own lot. It was always associated with Lot 6 even when it was part of Lot 1. The building was never specifically identified as a dwelling on the Sanborn maps, but the fact that it was assigned a street number suggests that it had residential rather than other uses.

No ancillary buildings or structures such as privies, wells, or sheds, were ever shown on the Sanborn maps. Possibly the Lot 17 residents used the privy in Lot 6 which was located at the east end of the Lot 17 building. This privy excavated in the course of this project, was designated Feature 10.

Lots 6 and 17: Owners and Residents

The history of lots 6 and 17 is inextricably interwoven, therefore they must be treated as a unit. Sources of information about property ownership and residency were the O'Quinn abstract tract books, city directories, and the 1900 and 1910 federal censuses. The directories and census data were the primary source for information about those residing on the lots over time. The directories were published on an occasional basis before about 1900 and therefore little information is available for the critical post-1900 years. The names in most of the directories are in alphabetical order, so a search of them to find who was living at a particular address, is a time consuming and mind numbing exercise that was not often performed. Tucson directories included listings on the basis of address only after 1917. Street addresses were shown on the federal census schedules from 1900, so matching names to street numbers was not possible before that year.

Ownership and residency was researched in detail only up to 1930. The primary reason for developing historical background information was to be able to match dated trash deposits with the residents of each lot. None of these deposits dated later than 1930. Over the years there were more nonresident owners than there were those who resided on their own property.

Although technically requiring references, the numerous specific citations needed for each of the dates, family names, and for other information, have purposefully not been included in the discussions for lots 6, 7, and 17 below. This omission was primarily for the sake of readability.

Information relating to property ownership came from the O'Quinn abstract track books and is summarized in Tables 2.4 and 2.5. Some data about ownership, rentals, and families came from the federal census schedules for 1900 and 1910. Most of the information about who was living at a particular lot when, was obtained from the 1881 to 1930 Tucson city directories.

Lot 6 was first sold by the Village of Tucson to Fritz Contzen in August 1872 (Table 2.4). In 1883 Contzen sold to Fred Maish who in turn sold to Thomas Driscoll in 1885. Six months later the property, now in the name of Sarah or Sena Driscoll was sold to John L. Brady in January 1896.

Grantor	Grantee	Date	Deed Book	Page	Listed Action
Village of Tucson	Fritz Contzen	8-2-1872	1	705	Deed
Contzen	F. Maish	6-8-1883	12	169	B&S
Maish	Thos. Driscoll	6-22-1885	13	154	B&S
Driscoll	Sena Driscoll	12-24-1885	13	583	Deed
D. Driscoll	J. L. Brady	1-20-1896	25	704	B&S
Richard Brady	Tucson Bldg. & Loan Assoc.	1-21-1896	13	46	Mtg.
Estate of Josephine L. Brady		5-12-1902	(Misc.)	568	Order
Richard Brady	J. H. Schneider	6-5-1902	34	72	Deed
J. H. Schneider	R. G. Brady	6-20-1902	34	141	Deed
Mrs. P. R. Brady	Providential Mutual Bldg & Loan Assoc.	2-18-1903	18	754	Mtg.
R.G. Brady	Mrs. P. R. Brady	2-20-1903	34	398	Deed
Mrs. P. R. Brady	Margaret Brady	1-18-1910	49	211	B&S
Prov. Mutual	Mrs. P. R. Brady	11-29-1911	12	66	Deed of Rel.
Margaret Brady	H. J. McQuigg	7-9-1913	56	113	W. D.
McQuigg	Margaret Brady	7-9-1913	36	108	Mtg.
McQuigg	Anita Williams	9-11-1919	21	386	Agr.
Anita Williams	Homestead	10-4-1924	1	302	H.S.
Guardian Invest. Co.	Anita Williams	9-21-1925	112	609	Deed
Anita Williams	Bernabe Robles	9-10-1926	70	250	Mtg.
McQuigg	Guaradian Invest. Company	9-26-1926	106	41	Deed
Anita W. Rochin	Bernable Robles	11-30-1928	84	445	Mtg.
B. Robles	Anita Williams	12-19-1928	#15471	Canceled	Mtg.
Anita Rochin	Teofilo Otero	2-17-1930	93	407	Mtg.
Anita Rochin	Bernabe Robles	2-18-1930	93	427	Mtg.
Teofilo Otero	MBC - E.Y.M.Jr.(?)	3-7-1930	93	407	Marginal Release

*Source: O'Quinn Abstract Tract Book, Special Collections, Main Library, University of Arizona

Table 2.4
Property Transactions in Lots 6 and 17

Grantor	Grantee	Date	Deed Book	Page	Listed Action
Village of Tucson	G. H. Oury	9-17-1872			Deed
G. H. Oury	L. M. Jacobs	7-30-1880	4	95	Mtg.
G. H. Oury	Jno. D. Walker	11-7-1885	7	192	Mtg.
G. H. Oury	Jno. D. Walker	10-28-1889	15	394	B&S
A. J. Doran, Admin.	E. Ochoa	1-9-1893	23	687	Deed
E. Ochoa	Leo Goldschmidt	1-12-1893	25	188	B & S
Goldschmidt	Chas. von Erxleben	9-15-1894	26	705	Deed
C. von Erxleben	L. Goldschmidt	9-15-1894	10	770	Mtg.
Chas. von Erxleben	Homestead	3-6-1895	1	86	H.S.
C. von Erxleben	Jane von Erxleben	10-1-1895	27	156	Deed
J. von Erxleben	E. G. Peacock	10-1-1895	12	107	Mtg.
Tax Collector	Lewis G. Davis	4-28-1903	34	529	Deed
Davis	Chas. Blenman	11-6-1903	34	765	Deed
J. von Erxleben	A. M. Franklin	5-25-1904	36	136	Deed
Chas. Blenman	A. M. Franklin	5-25-1904	36	134	Deed
P. B. T. Leigler Tr.	Jno. R. Gorby	11-18-1904	20	180	Mtg.
P. B. T. Leigler	R. Garstang	10-6-1905	20	670	Mtg.
City of Tucson	G. H. Oury	3-12-1907	42	178	Reissue of Deed
Sheriff	B. Maish	7-3-1907	42	429	Deed
L. Maish	B. Maish	12-19-1908	46	94	B & S
Sheriff (Jane von Erxleben & husband)	B. Maish	12-29-1908	44	642	Deed
B. Maish	Gabriel Roletti	1-27-1909	25	183	Mtg.
B. Maish	E. Aros	10-14-1909	47	669	Deed
Elvira Aros	So. Az. Bank & Tr.	11-9-1909	29	282	Mtg.
Annie Ochoa & husb.	Chas. Maish	9-8-1913	56	212	Q. C.
Esperanza Aros &wife	Helen Walker	1-19-1915	38	66	Mtg.
Elvira Aros, et al.	Minnie Cameron	6-19-1917	42	269	Mtg.
Elvira Aros, et al.	Bernabe Robles	3-31-1927	73	561	Mtg.

* Source: O'Quinn Abstract Tract Book, Special Collections, Main Library, University of Arizona

Table 2.5

Property Transactions in Lot 7

A survey of the city directories indicates that many of the early owners of Lot 6 did not reside on the lot. Fritz Contzen, the first private owner, was living on the property in 1881 as was a Joseph Browder. In 1883 the directory reports Contzen on Lot 6 along with Ramon Heredia's fruit store. Who lived on the property between 1872 and 1881 is unknown, but the house may not have been built until about 1881.

It was at the time of the 1896 sale, that part of Lot 1 became Lot 17, and was included as part of Lot 6. Lot 17 was located on the west side of Lot 6. The two lots continued to be sold as a unit throughout the history of the property at least up to 1930.

The purchase of the lots by John Brady in 1896 began a relatively long history of ownership by various members of the Brady family. John and R. G. Brady lived on the lot from about 1896 to 1899 when they moved to another location.

The Peter Brady family took up residency at least as early as 1900, the year they are listed in the census as living at 304 South Meyer Street. Probably they began living on Lot 6 in 1899 when they moved to Tucson and when the other Brady's left it. In the beginning Peter rented from his relatives.

Peter Brady was a pioneer who came to Arizona in 1854 (Tucson Daily Citizen February 10, 1919). According to the 1900 census, he was 74 years old and his occupation was listed as miner. He was married to Antonia, his third wife, who was born in Mexico. His first two wives were also of Mexican descent. Brady had three sons, John, Charles, and James, and a daughter, Margaret, by his second wife. An adopted daughter, Josephine, and a niece, Rosa Lopez, from Mexico also resided with the family. Peter died in 1902, and his wife acquired the lots through purchase in 1903. In that year the house was occupied by the family plus Robert Dunlaney, who may have been a boarder. In 1910 the house was occupied by Antonia, Margaret, Charles, James, Josephine, and Morganila Acuna, Antonia's sister. When Antonia died probably in late 1910, the children inherited the lots and house and continued to live there until the property was sold in 1913.

After 1913, lots 6 and 17 were sold to a succession of Anglo owners, and after the mid-1920s to individuals of Mexican descent. Residents of the house on Lot 6 after 1913 were mostly Mexican although Anglos lived there from 1920 to 1922. Other than their names, no information was located about these individuals.

Lot 7: Building History

Lot 7, like its neighbor Lot 6, was designated as such when the town was laid out in 1872. The shape of this lot was roughly rectangular in plan; it extended east-west across the entire width of Block 228. The lot was approximately 267 ft. long east-west on its north and south sides, 87 ft. wide north-south on its west end, and about 86 ft. wide at its east end.

This lot fronted on two major streets, Main on the west and Meyer on the east. As a result of its location Lot 7 had a more complex history of use than did lots 6 and 17. Fortunately the west end of the lot can be characterized as exhibiting very little change over time. It was this part of the lot that contained several excavated features.

Because Lot 7 was a complete entity in itself, no interior dividing lines would be expected. Also the property ownership records do not indicate that there was any division of the lot through time. In practice, however, some separation of the space between dwellings seems to have occurred. To reinforce the unity of the lot, a 10 ft. high wall was in place at its east edge along Meyer Street from about 1883 to sometime between 1896 and 1901.

The house on Lot 7 facing South Main Street was designated 313 on the Sanborn maps from 1883 to 1896. Sometime between 1896 and 1901 the house number was changed to 315 South Main Street, a number which it retained until it was demolished in 1968. The year this house was built could not be determined.

The 1883 Sanborn map shows no interior divisions, however the 1886, 1889, and 1896 maps indicate that a fence was erected east of the Main Street house giving it about a 100 ft. deep east-west space from the street. This fence ran along the east side of the privy which was designated Feature 7 during excavation of this area. All of the Lot 7 features were found between the rear of the house and this fence, or within an east-west distance of about 40 ft.

Later, the Sanborn maps from 1901, 1909, and 1914, indicate a division of the lot into a much deeper space that extended about 175 ft. from Main Street. From 1919 to 1947 no interior fences were shown on the Sanborn maps.

From at least 1883 to 1886 the Main Street house was the only house on Lot 7. It was a rectangular adobe building approximately 40 ft. east-west and 50 ft. north-south in size. A wood fence porch or shed was attached to its rear, or east side. Remarkably, this building survived for over 85 years, virtually unchanged until 1968 when it was demolished.

The 1886 map indicates that a long, wood frame building was added at the southeast corner of the lot on South Meyer Street. This building was about 12 ft. wide north-south and 70 ft. long east-west. It was designated 432 1/2 the primary number being that of the building in the next lot to the south. Although the building was on Lot 7 it may have been used by the residents of the lot to the south.

By 1896 the 70 ft. long building was gone. In this year a smaller combination adobe and wood frame building was illustrated along the south side of the lot about midway between the two streets. The adobe part of the building was about 12 ft. by 20 ft. and the wood frame about 12 ft. by 32 ft. The adobe remained on the lot until after 1919, the frame building was removed sometime between 1914 and 1919.

A small adobe building was added about 1901 at mid lot opposite the buildings on the south side of the lot. It was about 15 ft. by 27 ft. in size with its long axis east-west along the lot line. With the construction of this building there were three buildings on the block, one facing Main Street and two midblock until sometime between 1909 and 1914. At this time the building at midblock on the north side of the lot was demolished.

Sometime between 1909 and 1914 the first house that faced South Meyer Street was built. This was an adobe building about 27 ft. east-west and 35 ft. north-south. Between 1914 and 1919 several changes were made on the east part of Lot 7. The house on Meyer Street was expanded by adding about 12 ft. to its south side and a frame porch was added to the length of its west side. The wood frame building attached to the small adobe on the south lot line at midlot was removed and between the adobe and the Meyer Street house four small adobe buildings were constructed. Overall these covered an area about 20 ft by 50 ft.

In 1918 a commercial building, the Royal Theater, was constructed in the northeast corner of the lot. The theater faced South Meyer Street and was about 30 ft. wide and 140 ft. long east-west. The theater was built of brick and had a stage and scenery area on its west end. This part of the building was wood frame covered with corrugated iron. The buildings that were on Lot 7 by 1918 remained until at least 1952 according to the Sanborn maps. All the major buildings on the lot were there until 1968 when they were demolished to make room for construction of the Convention Center.

Lot 7: Owners and Residents

As with lots 6 and 17, the city directories, the federal census, and the O'Quinn abstract tract books were relied upon for information concerning the owners and residents of Lot 7. This information was researched only up to 1930. Potential citations were treated in the same manner as for lots 6 and 17 in that only general references, rather than specific citations, are provided for each of the dates mentioned.

Property transactions for Lot 7 from 1872 to 1930 are summarized in Table 2.5. Information used to compile this table came from the O'Quinn abstract tract books. The federal census for 1900 and 1910 provided additional family names. Names of lot residents and their dates of residency were obtained from the various city directories.

The documented history of Lot 7, Block 228, begins in 1872 when G. H. Oury purchased it from the Village of Tucson. Between 1880, when Oury first sold it by taking a mortgage on it, and 1894, the property experienced a number of changes in ownership, all but one of which involved individuals who can be classified as Anglos. In 1894 the lot was purchased by Charles von Erxleben, a civil and mining engineer, who in 1901 was the U.S. Deputy Mineral Surveyor. Von Erxleben may have been the first owner of the lot to live on it. The von Erxleben family retained ownership of the lot until 1904 and had some connection with it until 1808 (Table 2.5). The only other pre-1900 resident of the the lot, whose name is known, was Joe Phy who lived there in 1881. Phy was an employee of the city water works.

According to the 1900 census, the von Erxleben household consisted of Charles, aged 52, who was born in Germany and his wife Jennie, aged 40, who was born in England. They had two children, a daughter Hildebert, aged 9, and a son Edward, aged 6. In addition to the family, C. Elliot, aged 78, was listed in the census as a boarder and Albert Reder, aged 69, was listed as a servant in the household.

According to the 1903 directory, in addition to the von Erxleben's, C. F. Chapman, W. B. Chapman, and F. O. Emerson occupied the house at 315 South Main Street. Whether these individuals were boarders or whether the house had been divided into apartments by 1903 is unknown. Sanborn first labels the house as a "tenement", that is an apartment building, on the 1919 map, a classification it enjoyed until at least 1951.

Jennie (or Jane or Jeannie) von Erxleben is listed as a grantor, along with the sheriff, as late as 1908 but the 1903 directory is the last indication that the von Erxlebens occupied the property. They are not listed in the 1906 or 1908 directories.

Other than a brief involvement by E. Ochoa as a grantee-grantor in 1893, no person of Mexican descent was connected to 315 South Main Street until about 1907 when Bacilia Maish appears to have acquired the lot. Subsequently several individuals of Mexican background were involved with Lot 7 (Table 2.5).

The city directories, although they do not necessarily represent a complete listing of the occupants of 315 South Main Street, suggest that other than the Von Erxlebens, none of the owners up to 1930 who are listed as grantees or grantors in Table 2.5 were residents of the lot. Individuals of Mexican descent were residents on the lot almost exclusively according to the city directories. The city directories often, but not always, list several individuals as resident in the house after 1903. In 1910 Enrique Roma and his family of three and Emilio Noriega and his family of eight were renting apartments at the house, according to the census of that year. From 1917 to 1919 three or more individuals resided there. By 1920 the house appears to have reverted to a single family home again, a status maintained at least to 1935.

The Lot 7 property ownership records do not distinguish between the west and east parts of the lot. Presumably the adobe house at 322 South Meyer Street, which was built sometime about 1912, and the Royal Theater built in 1918, both on the east side of Lot 7, were owned by those who owned the house at 315 South Main Street. The city directories indicate that Esperanza Aros and his wife Elvira lived at 322 South Meyer Street from about 1912 to at least 1935. They apparently acquired Lot 7 in 1909.

No information was located as to who owned, leased, or rented the Royal Theater building. The theater ceased having live performances about 1935 and was used as a movie house for many years afterwards.

Chapter 3

FEATURES: BLOCK 228, LOTS 6 AND 17

Lot 6

Lot 6 features (Fig. 3.1) will be discussed here first. They are also shown on figures. 1.2 and 1.3

Feature 1

Feature 1 was a small basin shaped trash pit remnant found in the north end of Trench 5 during testing. Historically the pit was located in the northwest corner of Lot 17. During testing the backhoe cut through the east side of the pit leaving only a trace of it in the east wall of the trench. The majority of what remained was found in the west trench wall.

The pit remnant in the west wall was 39 in. long north-south and it extended westward about 18 in. Its overall east-west length was originally about 42 in., making it a nearly square pit. No sidewalls for the pit could be discerned beyond about 9.5 in. above its base. The base of the pit was 37 in. below the ground surface after the removal of the parking lot paving.

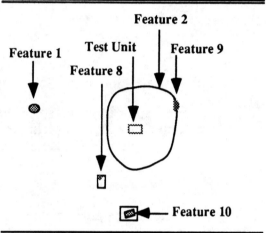

Figure 3.1
Lots 6 and 17 Archaeological Features

The upper 24 in. of the fill above the pit appeared to have been disturbed, redeposited fill containing numerous caliche nodules and a large basalt rock. This fill was redeposited here during construction of the Tucson Convention Center. Only about 3.5 in. of undisturbed, relatively artifact free fill, lay over the pit remnant. This fill was a dark brown, sandy soil mixed with a few charcoal flecks and very small artifact fragments.

Only the 4.5 in. thick ash, charcoal, and artifact layer at the base of the pit was excavated. This was accomplished by digging into the west wall of the trench. The ash and charcoal probably were from stove ashes.

Other than a brief use as a trash repository no function could be assigned this feature. It was not a latrine.

Artifacts

A total of 59 whole and fragmentary artifacts representing 26 individual objects were recovered from Feature 1 (Table 3.1).

Food

A milk bottle embossed "THATCHER MFG. CO." on its base is the only food artifact from Feature 1. This bottle dates 1900 to 1946 (Toulouse 1971: 496).

Material	Food	FP&C	HF	Personal	T&H	L&R	Unid.	Total
Glass	1		1			18	1	21
Ceramic		2						2
Metal					1			1
Other				1			1	2
Total	1	2	1	1	1	18	2	26

Table 3.1
Feature 1 Artifacts by Function

Food Preparation and Consumption

In this category are a hardpaste white earthenware ceramic form with a decal decoration and a Papago plain jar. The unidentifiable decal decorated form was made by Hughes, 1930-1935   (Godden 1964: 340).

Household Furnishings

A kerosene lamp chimney is the lone furnishings artifact.

Leisure and Recreation

Leisure and Recreation artifacts are a wine bottle, a machine made, crown finished, Obear-Nester manufactured beer bottle, and 16 machine made, wine finished liter sized bottles. The beer bottle dates 1915 to the present (Toulouse 1971: 374). The 16 liter sized bottles are grey green, yellow green, aqua, clear, and green in color. All were made on an Owens machine and were roughly finished. Two have the mark of Vidreria Monterey on their bases, 1909 to the present (Toulouse 1971: 518; Fontana 1968: 48). Given that all 16 appear to be of the same quality they may all have been made in Mexico. Although they look like wine bottles they may all have contained tequila.

Personal

A shoe is the only artifact with a personal function.

Tools and Hardware

A small, loop handled screwdriver of the type frequently included with a sewing machine falls into this functional category.

Unidentified

Two artifacts, a clear glass bottle with an Illinois Glass Company mark on its base, 1916-1929 (Toulouse 1971: 264), and a piece of rubber hose could not be assigned a specific function.

Summary Feature 1

With so few datable artifacts, dating of this feature is general; the trash in it appears to date sometime around 1929 to 1930 (Fig.3.2).

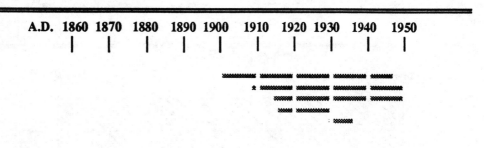

Figure 3.2

Feature 1 Artifact Date Ranges

No positive association between the trash and the occupation of Lot 17 can be made. According to the Sanborn maps, there were no buildings remaining on this lot after about 1919 to 1922; all had been demolished. It may be that the trash in Feature 1 was deposited by the occupants of the dwelling on Lot 6.

The trash appears to have a domestic habitation origin. The presence of stove ashes, food, food preparation and consumption, personal, the sewing machine screwdriver, and the leisure and recreation artifacts support this conclusion. The latter artifacts suggest the possibility that a heavy drinker was involved.

Feature 2

The second feature designated during testing was discovered between trenches 3 and 16 (Fig. 3.1). This was a large trash filled depression that was at least 34 ft. east-west and 43 ft. north-south in extent. The relatively shallow deposit extended over parts of both Lot 6 and Lot 17, although most of it was in Lot 6.

The depression was a receptacle for trash over a period of years. Irregular and discontinuous layers or lenses of sheet trash were built up to a depth of from 24 in. to 30.5 in. Overlying the undisturbed trash deposit were 16 in. of mixed, redeposited caliche and soil from the construction of the Tucson Convention Center. Construction of the center and the parking lot resulted in the removal of the upper part of the deposit, but exactly how much is unknown. The base of the deposit was from 40 in. to 46.5 in. below the ground surface remaining after the removal of the parking lot paving.

This deposit had been partially disturbed over the years by residents of the block and subsequently by construction of the center. Steam pipe and electrical line trenches were located on the north and east sides of the deposit which may have obscured the feature in those directions. Postconstruction tree wells also impacted parts of the historic trash.

Excavation of Feature 2 began with the removal, by backhoe, of the redeposited caliche layer below the parking lot paving to immediately above the top of the undisturbed trash. An area 6 ft. north-south and 7 ft. 8 in. east-west between backhoe trenches 2 and 15 that was relatively intact was selected for excavation.

The feature was excavated in three strata of one level each (Fig. 3.3). The levels were slightly deeper on the north end than on the south. S1-L1 was from 11 in. to 15.5 in. thick, S2-L1 was from 2 in. to 5 in. thick, and S3-L1 was a uniform 10 in. thick.

All three levels consisted of a dark grey brown, sandy clay, containing numerous artifacts and small pockets or lenses of ash and charcoal beginning in S2-L1. The base of S1-L1 was a thin lens of reddish sterile soil overlying a thin lens of caliche that extended across all but the northernmost 6 in. of the level. Both lenses were sterile. A thin ash and charcoal lens was at the base of S2-L1. The feature bottomed on hard, sterile caliche, which formed the base of S3-L1.

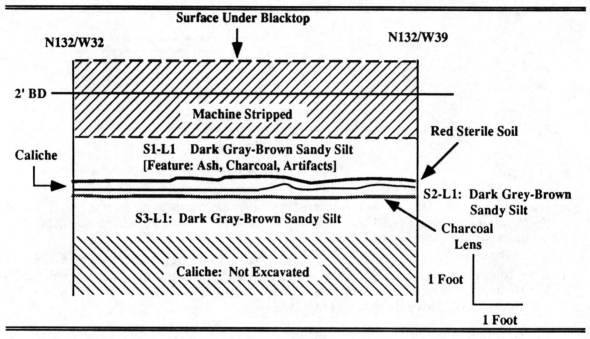

Figure 3.3
Feature 2 Profile

At the bottom of S3-L1 were bases of two postholes spaced about 3 ft. apart. One was 6 in. in diameter and 4 in. deep and one was 8 in. in diameter and 7 in. deep. The purpose of these was not established, but they may have been part of a non-property boundary fence.

On the west edge of the excavated area was a tree well that had been cut through by Trench 15. The top of the tree well was first recognized about 1 ft. below the surface. It had been covered over by construction fill. The well measued about 3.5 ft. north-south and 16 in. east-west and about 20 in. deep. The bottom of the well cut into the caliche layer below the layer of cultural debris. Given its stratigraphic position, this tree well was in use before the parking lot and Convention Center were constructed.

Artifacts

A total of 1506 whole and fragmentary artifacts representing a minimum of 402 individual items came from Feature 2. Seventeen were from the backhoe trenching, 79 from S1-L1, 98 from S2-L1, and 208 from S3-L1. These are listed by function in Table 3.2.

S1-L1 produced two unmarked food bottles, one of which appears to be relatively recent. A fruit jar came from S2-L1, and a fruit jar, and two unmarked pickle or condiment bottles were from S3-L1. Oyster shells were found in S1-L1 (4), S2-L1 (3), S3-L1 (1), and in the backhoe spoil (1).

Food Preparation and Consumption

A total of 177 artifacts are food preparation and consumption related (Table 3.3). These include both glass (2) and ceramic (175) forms used both in the kitchen and on the table. The majority is tableware.

Included in this tabulation are green glazed Mexican redware, and plain and red slipped Papago pottery. In both cases, bowl and jar forms predominate.

	Food	FP&C	HF	Arch	L&R	M&H	Pers.	Trans	T&H	Misc	Unid	Total
Backdirt												
Glass					1						2	3
Ceramic		12										12
Metal									1			1
Other	1											1
Total	1	12	0	0	1	0	0	0	1	0	2	17
S1-L1												
Glass	2	1		1	4	1	1					13
Ceramic		22		1								23
Metal				3	3				16	5	1	28
Other	4			1	1		1			6	2	15
Total	6	23	0	6	8	1	2	0	16	11	6	79
S2-L1												
Glass	1			1	7	2	1				1	13
Ceramic		42	1	1							2	46
Metal					4		2		16	1	4	27
Other	3						4			3	2	12
Total	4	42	1	2	11	2	7	0	16	4	9	98
S3-L1												
Glass	3	1			7	4	9			1	3	28
Ceramic		99	2	1	4						1	107
Metal			1		4		4	6	32	2	5	57
Other	1				1		7			8	2	19
Total	4	100	3	1	16	4	20	6	32	11	11	208
Total	15	177	4	9	36	7	29	6	65	26	28	402

Table 3.2
Feature 2 Artifacts by Function

All of the 17 artifacts found with the backhoe came from Trench 15 in the vicinity of the Feature 2 excavation, but not necessarily from it. A piece of SCA glass, 1880 to 1919 (Ayres 1984: 128) and a machine made bottle dating 1903 to the present, were the only datable artifacts from the backhoe activity.

Food

Material		Form	Backdirt	S1-L1	S2-L1	S3-L1	Total
Glass		Dinner Tumbler				1	1
		Stemware		1			1
Ceramic	Hardpaste White Earthenware	Small Plate	1		1	6	8
		Soup Plate				1	1
		Plate	1				1
		Bowl	1	1	1	9	12
		Cup	1		2	4	7
		Saucer		1	2	6	9
		Lid				1	1
		Handle	1				1
		Unid.	5	7	8	12	32
	Porcelain	Bowl				1	1
		Saucer				1	1
	Softpaste Earthenware	Mexican Forms	1	6	16	36	59
		Papago Forms	1	5	12	22	40
		Unid.		2			2
Total			12	23	42	100	177

Table 3.3

Feature 2   Food Preparation and Consumption Artifacts

Five Mexican redware forms and nine Papago forms are bowls with sooted bottoms indicating their use in cooking.

In S2-L1 is a possible saucer with an interior turquoise colored glaze. In S3-L1 is a yellow green sponge decorated form, two bowls and two cups of banded ware, a saucer and a platter (?) with a blue transfer printed decoration, a bowl with a purple transfer printed design, and plate with a red transfer printed design. All these forms are hardpaste white earthenwares.

Datable artifacts in this category are a Cochran made plate from S2-L1 dating 1846 to 1918 (Godden 1964: 158), a Meakin made saucer, plate, and unidentifiable form dating 1875 to 1897 (Godden 1964: 425), a Hughes plate, 1860 to 1894, (Godden 1964: 339), a gold band or line on a porcelain bowl and a saucer said by Kovel and Kovel (1986: 257) to date after 1876, and a McNichol plate dating 1892-1920 (Lehner 1980: 105), all from S3-L1. A turned pink stemware glass from S1-L1 dates ca. 1919 to the 1940s (see Giarde 1980: 164).

Household Furnishings

A Mexican made unglazed redware candlestick holder (S2-L1), a ceramic figurine, an upholstery tack, and a Mexican made green glazed redware flower pot (S3-L1) are classified as household furnishings.

Architecture

Only nine architecture related artifacts came from Feature 2. From S1-L1 are two roofing nails, a piece of window pane, a fired adobe brick of the type found in features 4, 5, and 11, and two hard rubber light bulb sockets. A piece of a window pane and a fired adobe brick (as above) were found in S2-L1, and a fired adobe brick (as above) came from S3-L1.

Leisure and Recreation

The 36 artifacts classified in this category are detailed in Table 3.4. These include alcoholic beverages (20), toys (5), firearm related (10), and a phonograph record.

	Alcoholic Beverages					Toys		Firearms			Other	Total
	Beer	Wine	Ale	Liquor	Whiskey Bottle Lid	Doll Dish	Lime-stone Marble	Rifle Action	Cap	Cart-ridge	Phono Record	
Backdirt		1										1
S1-L1	2	2			1					2	1	8
S2-L1	3	3		1						4		11
S3-L1	3	3		1		4	1	1	1	2		16
TOTALS	8	8	1	2	1	4	1	1	1	8	1	36

Table 3.4

Feature 2 Leisure and Recreation Artifacts

One of the beer bottles from S1-L1 is the only datable alcoholic beverage bottle. It was made by William McCully between 1872 to 1886 (Toulouse 1971: 351).

All of the eight cartridges are datable. In S1-L1 are two, possibly .32 Long, rimfire cartridges with "US " head stamps, 1875 to ca. 1900 (Barnes 1972: 80). The .44 caliber cartridge from S2-L1 dates 1873 to 1942 (Barnes 1972: 61) and the four .22 caliber cartridges with "H" head stamps from the same level date 1858-1940 (Logan 1959: 8).

Medical and Health

The seven artifacts in this category are five proprietary medicine bottles from S1-L1 (1), S2-L1 (1), and S3-L1 (3), and two prescription ware bottles, one each from S2-L1 and S3-L1. None were marked.

Personal

Of the 29 personal artifacts from Feature 2, two are from S1-L1, seven are from S2-L1, and 20 are from S3-L1.

From S1-L1 is a hard rubber fine toothed comb of the type illustrated in the 1897 Sears Roebuck & Co. catalog (Israel 1968: 326). It has "UNBREAKABLE" impressed in one side. A hair product embossed "CIRCASSIAN BLOOM" is also from S1-L1.

S2-L1 contained a mirror, a pen knife, a metal shoe toe clip, two shell and one bone buttons, and child's slate board.

Glass artifacts from S3-L1 are four glass buttons, a woman's glass coat button, and a crucifix and three glass beads, all from a rosary. S3-L1 metal artifacts are two shoe toe clips (parts of one clip), a match safe, and a button with a man's head on it. The other artifacts in this category are teeth from a hard rubber comb, a shoe, a slate pencil, three shell buttons, and a hard rubber hair brush back.

Transportation

All six of the artifacts in the transportation category are from S3-L1. These are two horse harness buckles, a harness O-ring, a harness chain link, and two horseshoes.

Tools and Hardware

A total of 65 artifacts were placed in this category. From the backhoe trench is a square cut nail. A Philips head screw, two pieces of iron wire, three machine bolts, and 10 wire nails are from S1-L1. S2-L1 produced 15 square cut nails and an iron washer. A piece of strap iron, a bolt, a piece of iron wire, a strap hinge, and 28 square cut nails are from S3-L1.

Miscellaneous

Twenty-six miscellaneous artifacts were recorded. In S1-L1 are a paper clip, three crown caps, a foil tube, a plastic screw cap, a prehistoric trough metate, two pieces of copper (?) ore, a piece of coal, and a flashlight battery core. From S2-L1 are one tin can and three pieces of copper (?) ore. S3-L1 contained a glass rod, two tin cans, two prehistoric manos, and six prehistoric pieces of lithic shatter or waste from flaking.

Unidentified

Twenty-eight artifacts are unidentified as to function. An SCA fragment dates 1880 to 1919 (Ayres 1984: 128) and a machine made piece of brown glass dates 1903 to the present. A number of relatively recent artifact fragments were found in S1-L1 and a piece of plastic was located in S2-L1.

Summary Feature 2

Given the presence of artifacts related to women and children, it is likely that some of the trash in Feature 2 resulted from its use by one or more families. These artifacts include a woman's coat button, four doll dishes, a toy marble, a school slate board, and a slate pencil. Except for the slate board from S2-L1, all of these artifacts came from S3-L1. This may indicate that only the trash in S3-L1 resulted from family use of the feature. If that is the case, the origin of S2-L1, and especially S1-L1, trash is from unknown sources; however, the absence of women's and children's artifacts in these strata does not preclude a family origin for the trash. According to the Sanborn maps, and other sources, the Lot 6 house was a dwelling at least from 1883 to about 1968.

In further support of the upper strata trash as family or domestic habitation deposits, one has only to look at the artifacts. Food, food preparation and consumption, personal, and leisure and recreation artifacts are found in all three strata.

Dating

Most of the 78 artifacts from S1-L1 were manufactured in historic times, but several were of relatively recent origin (Fig.3.4). This suggests that much of S1-L1 had been disturbed by demolition and subsequent construction of the Convention Center. The ground disturbance and mixing that occurred impacted all of Stratum 1 to, and probably including, the two sterile lenses at its base.

The "turned pink" stemware dating ca. 1919 to the 1940s, a light bulb socket, an aluminum whiskey bottle lid, a phonograph record, the wire, bolts, a screw, plastic, roofing nails, a paper clip, crown caps, and other artifacts were clearly of relatively recent origin. The idea that S1-L1 was disturbed and contained recent material is supported by the presence of a 1963 Lincoln penny reported in the field notes but not collected.

Pink glass results when the selenium additive in glass is exposed to ultra violet rays of the sun. Glass with selenium in it will turn either straw, or light pink in color, hence the tentative use of the term "turned pink" for this glass. The amount of selenium in the glass probably determines which color will be produced.

Giarde (1980: 164-165) dates pink glass to post-1910. He dates straw colored glass to 1914 to 1930, and Kendrick (1963: 45) dates it to the same years. Because selenium was used to replace manganese as a decolorizer in glass, it probably was not extensively used until about 1919. Therefore both straw and turned pink colored glass was probably not common until about 1919. Numerous examples of both colors are known into the 1940s.

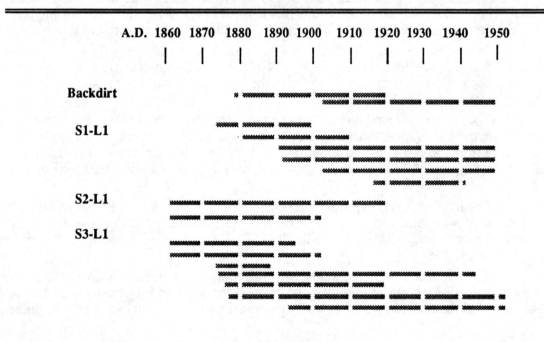

Figure 3.4
Feature 2 Artifact Date Ranges

Other datable artifacts from S1-L1 were a beer bottle of the type common between 1880 to 1910, two U.S. head stamped .32 Long cartridges, ca. 1875 to ca. 1900 Barnes 1972:80), and wire nails dating ca. 1890 to the present. S1-L1 was the only stratum with machine made bottles (1903 to the present). If we disregard the recent artifacts, the other datable artifacts in S1-L1 can all be accounted for within a date range of about 1900 to 1910.

An insufficient number of datable artifacts were recovered from S2-L1 to provide a meaningful date for this stratum.

Many of the dates obtained from S3-L1 artifacts are from ceramic maker's marks. All the datable artifacts can be subsumed within a date range of 1886 to 1900. The McCully beer bottle has an end date of 1886. If we assume that the bottle was reused, as was often the case, or that Toulouse's end is incorrect, then the bottle may have been in use into the 1890s. If so, then the date range accounting for all the artifacts in S3-L1 can be extended to about 1894 to 1900. The 1894 date is the end date for the Hughes made plate.

The beginning of the use of the Feature 2 area as a trash dump probably occurred before the subdivision of Lot 6 into lots 6 and 17. Subdivision took place sometime between 1896 and 1901 according to the Sanborn maps.

For the excavated part of this large feature, we can suggest that trash was first deposited there in the early 1890s up to about 1910, or for a period possibly as long as 16 years.

Within Feature 2 the majority of the trash, or 52 percent, was deposited in S3-L1. Thus this trash dump received most of its use prior to about 1900, after which time its use steadily declined.

Feature 8

A trash pit located in the south-central part of Lot 17 was designated Feature 8 (Fig. 3.1). This feature was discovered in Trench 14 during the testing phase of the project. The backhoe revealed the west edge of the feature, so little damage occurred to it.

Feature 8 was located only a few feet north of the front of the former frame dwelling in Lot 17 that was variously identified as 424 1/2, 304 1/2, and 300 1/2 South Meyer Street on the Sanborn maps. Given its proximity to the house it is unlikely to have been in use during the time the house was occupied.

The feature was irregular in form and extended to the east for some distance beyond the limits of the excavation. An arbitrary 3 ft. 8 in. by 6 ft. rectangular area was excavated eastward from the east trench to collect a sample of the cultural material it contained. The upper fill consisting of 14.2 in. of redeposited soil and caliche was first removed by the backhoe prior to hand excavation.

The hand excavation proceeded in two stages. First, the upper trashy fill overlying the pit remnant was removed in two levels, and second, the more limited area of pit fill was removed in one level. S1-L1 was 2 in. thick, S1-L2 was 3.5 in. to 5 in. thick and the pit, S2-L1, was 4 in. deep.

The pit was a narrow, shallow depression in an area of thin sheet trash. It was probably part of a large pit that had cut through the surrounding trashy fill. Because only a small part of the feature was excavated, its original purpose or full extent remain unclear.

Artifacts

Feature 8 produced a total of 340 whole and fragmentary artifacts representing a minimum of 118 individual objects: 16 from S1-L1 and 102 from S2-L1. No artifacts were found in S1-L2 (Table 3. 5).

Food

An oyster shell from S1-L1 and two machine made milk bottles, one of which is embossed "The Holstein Dairy" in script, ca. 1917-1932 (Tucson Directory Co. 1917; Arizona Directory Co. 1932: 531) from S2-L1 were found in Feature 8.

	Food	FP&C	HF	Arch	L&R	M&H	Personal	T&H	Misc	Unid	Total
S1-L1											
Glass										5	5
Ceramic		2									2
Metal				2					4		6
Other	1								1	1	3
Total	1	2	0	0	2	0	0	4	1	6	16
S2-L1											
Glass	2	6	1	2	9	4	2			8	34
Ceramic		21		2						1	24
Metal		1		1	1			30	4		37
Other					1		5		1		7
Total	2	28	1	5	11	4	7	30	5	9	102
Total	3	30	1	7	11	4	7	34	6	15	118

Table 3.5

Feature 8 Artifacts by Function

Food Preparation and Consumption

Thirty artifacts, two from S1-L1 and 28 from S2-L1, fall into this functional category (Table 3.6).

One of the hardpaste white earthenware saucers, the dinner plate, and one unidentified form were made by Homer Laughlin and date ca. 1909, ca. 1913, and ca. 1905 respectively (Gates and Ormerod 1982: 129, 133). One porcelain saucer that is labeled "HAND PAINTED IN JAPAN" probably dates ca. 1921-1940 (Stitt 1974: 176) and one with H & Co. on its base dates 1879 to the present (Kovel and Kovel 1986: 178). One of the Papago bowls has a sooted exterior and was obviously used for cooking purposes.

The softpaste earthenware plate has blue, red, green, and yellow glazes on it and is of the type known as majolica.

Household Furnishings

Only one artifact, an SCA kerosene lamp chimney, 1880-1919 (Ayres 1984: 128), could be classified under this function.

Architecture

A piece of window screen and a piece of cloth covered electrical wire came from S1-L1. From S2-L1 are two window glass panes, an electrical fixture, a piece of electrical wire, and a "BRUNT" ceramic insulator. The insulator dates 1892 to 1911 (Gates and Ormerod 1982: 19).

Material		Form	S1-L1	S1-L2	Total
Glass		Stemware		1	1
		Tumbler		4	4
		Pressed Glass Bowl		1	1
Ceramic	Hardpaste White Earthenware	Dinner Plate		1	1
		Saucer		3	3
		Cup		1	1
		Bowl		1	1
		Unidentified Form	2	2	4
	Porcelain	Saucer		2	2
		Cup		1	1
		Unidentified Form		1	1
	Softpaste Earthenware	Plate		1	1
		Jar		1	1
		Mexican Forms		2	2
		Papago Forms		5	5
Metal	Enamelware	Pan Handle		1	1
Total			**2**	**28**	**30**

Table 3.6
Feature 8 Food Preparation and Consumption Artifacts

Leisure and Recreation

Leisure and recreation artifacts, all from S2-L1, are seven beer bottles, a wine bottle, a liquor bottle, a lead foil finish cover from a wine or champagne bottle, and a celluloid doll. Most of the alcoholic beverage bottles were machine made and thus date after 1903. Two of the beer bottles were made by William Franzen and Sons, 1900 to 1929 (Toulouse 1971: 536).

Medicine and Health

There are two proprietary medicine bottles, one unmarked and one embossed "LISTERINE LAMBERT PHARMACAL COMPANY" with an Illinois Glass Company base mark. The marked bottle dates 1916 to 1929 (Toulouse 1971: 264). Two bottles are homeopathic vials.

Personal

Artifacts of a personal nature are two cologne or toilet water bottles, one of which was machine made, a shell collar stud, two shell clothing buttons, a shoe, and slate pencil. One of the bottles has "...PINAUD PARIS REGISTERED" on its side and "BOTTLE PROPERTY OF H & G REG KLOTZ & CO."

Tools and Hardware

Four wire nails (S1-L1), four square cut nails (1860 to 1900), 25 wire nails (1890 to present), and a piece of wire (S2-L1) were found in Feature 8.

Miscellaneous

The six miscellaneous artifacts are a prehistoric ground stone fragment from S1-L1, and a brass grommet, a bucket ear, a tin can, a threaded brass plug, and a seed, possibly a walnut, from S2-L1.

Unidentified

Fifteen artifacts, six from S1-L1 and nine from S2-L1, could not be identified as to function.

Feature 8 Summary

According to the Sanborn maps, the dwelling in Lot 17 was demolished sometime between 1919 and 1922. The artifacts from S2-L1 appear to date to the same time period, that is, about 1919 to 1921 (Fig.3.5). It is possible that the trash in Feature 8 was deposited there as a result of the demolition of the Lot 17 house. Three of the ceramic forms, the Brunt insulator, and the square cut nails predate the suggested date range. Because ceramics often survive for years after manufacture, they easily could have been in use into the 1920s. The square cut nails and the insulator could have been in use in the house before its removal.

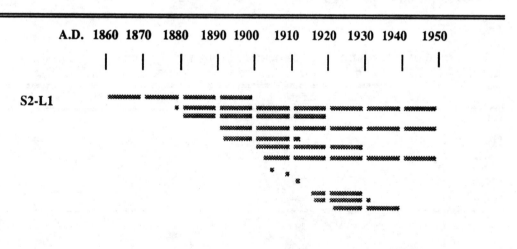

Figure 3.5

Feature 8 Artifact Date Ranges

S1-L1, under the redeposited caliche layer, contained plastic and brick probably from the demolition of the theater and other buildings in the vicinity in the late 1960s. No artifacts were found in S1-L2.

For the most part, the artifacts suggest that a family was responsible for the Feature 8 deposit. Among these were a milk bottle, ceramics, and children and women's artifacts. In the latter category were a doll, a slate pencil, and toilet water or cologne bottles.

Feature 9

Feature 9 was discovered near the north end of Trench 16 during the test excavations. The backhoe cut through the center of the feature, a circular, trash filled pit. It was located on the northeast edge of the large trash filled depression of which Feature 2 was also a part. As with Feature 2, Feature 9 was in the northwest quarter of Lot 6 (Fig. 3.1).

The edges of the pit were noticeable only below the redeposited soil and caliche placed there during construction of the Convention Center and parking lot. This 18.6 in. thick layer was removed with pick and shovel down to a level about 8 in. above the top of the pit. This layer of highly organic, trash filled, dark sandy clay, was removed to the pit top as Stratum 1. The 20 in. deep pit remnant was excavated as Stratum 2. It contained the same type of fill as Stratum 1. Only that part of the pit on the eastside of Trench 16 was excavated.

Originally the pit was between 6 ft. to 7 ft. in diameter. It had irregular, sloping sides and a relatively flat bottom coincident with the top of the caliche bed. The pit's north-south dimension measured 70 in, and it extended 20.5 in. to the east.

It is unclear why the pit edge was not discernable above Stratum 2. Most likely it was present in Stratum 1 but could not be seen because of the similarity in the color and nature of the fill to the surrounding deposits.

The shape and size of the pit and the presence of a rotted tree stump in the Stratum 1 level suggests that the pit was a tree well dug into the underlying trash deposits. When refilled the formerly stratified trash was mixed. The pit would have been excavated sometime prior to the demolition of the buildings on Lot 6 and the construction of the Convention Center (that is sometime before the late 1960s) by the owner of Lot 6. Preparation of the area for a parking lot removed the upper part of the pit.

Artifacts

A total of 330 whole and fragmentary artifacts representing a minimum of 89 individual items, 30 from S1-L1 and 59 from S2-L1, came from Feature 9 (Table 3.7).

	Food	FP&C	HF	Arch	L&R	M&H	Personal	T&H	Misc	Unid	Total
S1-L1											
Glass	2			1	1					2	6
Ceramic		12			1						13
Metal							1	5	2	1	9
Other									2		2
Total	2	12	0	1	2	0	1	5	4	3	30
S2-L1											
Glass	1	2	1		3	5	4		1	2	19
Ceramic		20									20
Metal			1				2	17			20
Other											0
Total	1	34	2	1	5	5	7	22	5	5	89
Total	3	34	2	1	5	5	7	22	5	5	89

Table 3.7

Feature 9 Artifacts by Function

Food

A condiment or pickle bottle and a machine made fruit jar from S1-L1 and a "GILLET CHICAGO" extract bottle from S2-L1 constitute the Feature 9 food related artifacts. The extract bottle dates from 1873 to at least 1910 (Zumwalt 1980: 172).

Leisure and Recreation

In this category are a toy cup and beer bottle from S1-L1 and a wine bottle, a soda bottle, and an eye from a stuffed toy animal from S2-L1.

Material		Form	S1-L1	S2-L1	Total
Glass		Tumbler		2	2
Ceramic	Hardpaste White Earthenware	Peasantware Plate	1		1
		Peasantware Cup	1		1
		Cup	1	2	3
		Banded Bowl	1		1
		Unidentified Form	3	3	6
	Porcelain	Kaga Redware	1		1
		Unidentified Fkorm	1		1
	Softpaste Earthenware	Mexican Forms		6	6
		Papago Forms	3	9	12
TOTAL			12	22	34

Table 3.8

Feature 9 Food Preparation and Consumption Artifacts

Medical and Health

The three proprietary medicine and two prescription bottles, all unmarked, came from S2-L1.

Personal

The personal artifacts were a man's 18 k gold ring from S1-L1 and four milk glass buttons, a shoe lacing eyelet, and a metal button from S2-L1.

Tools and Hardware

Five nails unidentifiable as to type from S1-L1 and four square cut and 13 wire nails from S2-L1 represent the total tools and hardware artifacts.

Miscellaneous

S1-L1 produced four miscellaneous artifacts, a tin can, a friction cap from a powder (such as talcum) can, a piece of copper (?) ore, and a prehistoric flake. S2-L1 contained only a piece of SCA pressed glass of unidentifiable form dating 1880-1919 (Ayres 1984: 128).

Unidentified

Three artifacts, unidentifiable as to function, came from S1-L1, including a piece of SCA glass, dated as above. Two pieces of glass of unidentifiable form came from S2-L1.

Summary Feature 9

On Sanborn maps Feature 9 falls within the northwest corner of Lot 6. The trash in the pit, originally a tree well, was derived from the larger trash layer of which Feature 2 is a part. The artifacts appear to reflect a domestic origin, probably originating with the occupants of the house on this lot. The toy animal eye and the doll cup suggest the presence of at least one child and thus a family.

Dating

Few artifacts from Feature 9 were datable. Those that were include SCA glass (1880-1919), the Gillet extract bottle (1873 to 1910+), the Kaga redware (1850 to the present), machine made glass bottles (1903-1950), square cut nails (ca. 1860-1900), and wire nails (1890 to the present). Together these suggest a feature date of above 1900-1903, or slightly later. Because Feature 2 trash is also from this deposit, it is not surprising that the artifacts in Feature 9 and Feature 2 appear to be contemporaneous.

Feature 10

During the testing phase a trash filled pit was found in Trench 15. It was a roughly east-west oriented privy pit located in the southwest corner of Lot 6 between the house designated 424, and later 304 and 300, South Meyer Street, and the house to the west of it, in the rear, on Lot 17 (see Fig. 3.1).The privy was plotted only on the 1896 Sanborn map. This suggests a relatively short existence for this feature.

Overlying the pit was the redeposited caliche layer found throughout the project area and under this was a layer of historic trash mixed with some demolition period material such as fragments of plastic. Under the caliche layer evidence of pit subsidence was noted in the backhoe trench walls in S1-L1 and S1-L2. Trash dating after the privy was no longer used may have been deposited in the depression created by slumping.

The privy pit proper was first noticed in S1-L2 at the top of the naturally deposited caliche. The top of the privy pit probably began above the natural caliche layer, possibly in S1-L2 or even higher. Because the evidence for subsidence extends to the top of S1-L1, the top of the privy pit may have been cut off by demolition and construction activity.

The first stratum began about 8 in. below the surface after the removal of the parking lot paving. S1-L1 was about 8 in. in depth and S1-L2 was about 7 in. in depth. S1-L2 was the first level clearly within the confines of the privy pit. S2-L1 and S2-L2 were both 2 ft. levels. The final level S2-L3 was a shallow irregular level that covered only part of the pit. At its deepest, it was 10 in. thick, primarily because of a 6 in. deep, 16 in. diameter, depression at the east end of the privy floor. The privy floor was about 6 ft. 9 in. below the present surface. The privy pit was at least 5 ft. 5 in. in depth. Its upper dimensions were about 4 ft. by 7 ft. and at the base it narrowed to about 2.5 ft. by 5 ft.

Reference was made in the field notes to two small, apparently intrusive pits, one dug into the east and the other into the west edges of the privy. These were not distinguishable until excavation was nearly completed, but it was noted that they contained trash that dated later in time than that in the surrounding pit. The small pit on the west end contained burned trash and terminated in S2-L1. Each pit was about 12 in. to 13 in. in diameter. These pits may be the reason why several post 1900 artifacts were found in S2-L1 an otherwise pre 1900 feature.

Artifacts

Feature 10 produced 3976 whole and fragmentary artifacts representing a minimum of 1230 individual objects (Table 3.9). Additionally, 473 whole and fragmentary faunal remains were recovered (Table 3.10).

Food

Only 62 artifacts could be classified as food related (Table 3.11). Table 3.12 shows the food related animal bone, 116 pieces, from Feature 10. All the bone from Feature 10 was identified and analyzed.

Of the 116 pieces of food related faunal remains, 52 percent are beef bones which were found in every level of Feature 10. At least two individuals are represented. Included are five beef foot bones which probably were used to make menudo. Four of these were found in S1-L2 and one was in S2-L2. Other butchering units included the neck, front shank, shoulder, ribs, short loin, sirloin, rump, round, and hind shank. These represent nearly a complete animal and include both the inexpensive and the more costly cuts of meat.

Butchering units for the pig are feet, ham, and loin and for the sheep the leg, loin, and rack were represented.

Probably many of the 333 bones listed in Table 3.12 as small to large mammals and as unidentified are from beef and other food related animals. At least 58 bones in the mammal category and 22 in the unidentified category show evidence of butchering. Thirty-five bones in the mammal category and 17 unidentified were burned or calcined.

S1-L1

The five food artifacts in this level are a fruit jar, a 32 oz. food bottle, two milk bottles, and a peach seed. Chicken and beef remains also were found in this level.

S1-L2

Only four food artifacts, a machine-made milk bottle, a jelly jar, and two general food bottles, were found in Level 2. One of the food bottles is 32 oz. in size and one is a Durkee's sauce container dating from the 1850s to ca. 1929 (Zumwalt 1980: 129). Two tin cans could not be specifically identified as food containers, but may have been. They are listed under the Miscellaneous category as are those mentioned below.

Both chicken and beef remains were found in this level.

S2-L1

Twelve food containers were recovered in Level 1 of this stratum. These are two catsup bottles, nine general food bottles, and a milk bottle. One of the catsup bottles is embossed "THE T.A. SNIDER PRESERVE CO." which dates 1884 to ca. 1923 (Zumwalt 1980: 388; Toulouse 1971: 450). The other is an unmarked, machine made bottle dating from 1903.

	Food	FP&C	HF	M&H	Arch.	L&R	Pers.	Trans.	T&H	Comm	Misc.	Unid.	Total
S1-L1													
Glass	4	2		5	1	6						6	24
Ceramic		35	1		1							1	38
Metal									56		1	2	59
Other	1					1	1				3	1	7
Total	5	37	1	5	2	7	1	0	56	0	4	10	128
S1-L2													
Glass	4	4		3	1	2	1					10	25
Ceramic		46	3		1							2	52
Metal		1		1	1				51			126	60
Other							1				6	7	
Total	4	51	3	0	2	4	2	0	51	0	6	18	144
S2-L1													
Glass	12	37	9	28	6	8	33			3		22	158
Ceramic		36	2		1	4							43
Metal		1	3		1	3	15		89			12	124
Other		1					21				12	7	41
Total	12	75	14	28	8	15	69	0	89	3	12	41	366
S2-L2													
Glass	34	32	16	112	12	21	74			3	1	15	320
Ceramic		63	2		2	30				1			98
Metal	7	2	2		1	10	27	2	43		3	16	113
Other							44			1	4		49
Total	41	97	20	112	15	61	145	2	43	5	8	31	580
S2-L3													
Glass		1	1	2		1						1	6
Ceramic		3				2							5
Metal													0
Other							1						1
Total	0	4	1	2	0	3	1	0	0	0	0	1	12
Total	62	264	39	151	28	88	218	2	239	8	30	101	1230

Table 3.9
Feature 10 Artifacts by Function

FOOD SPECIES	NO. OF INDIVIDUALS	NO. OF BONES				
		S1-L1	S1-L2	S2-L1	S2-L2	Total
Gallus gallus (Chicken)	3	2	6	0	9	17
Bos taurus (Beef)	2	2	24	24	10	60
Ovis/Capra (Sheep or Goat)		0	0	6	11	7
Telecost (Bony Fish)		0	0	11	3	14
Anatinae (Duck)		0	0	2	0	2
Sus scrofa (Pig)	1	0	0	5	0	5
Eggshell (Chicken)		0	0	0	1	1
TOTAL		4	30	48	34	116
OTHER						
Aves (Unidentified bird)		0	1	0	2	3
Rodentia (Unidentified rodent)		0	0	1	0	1
Neotoma albigula (White throated wood rat)	2	0	0	5	5	
Neotoma sp. (Wood rat)		0	0	0	15	15
Small to large unidentified mammals		21	63	69	36	189
Unidentified		10	32	62	40	144
TOTAL		31	96	137	93	357

Table 3.10

Feature 10 Faunal Remains

The nine general food containers whose contents are unknown, are all hand finished. Five of these are bottles of 32 oz. capacity. One has "CS & Co." on its base. This is the mark of Cannington Shaw and Company, an English food bottle maker, ca. 1875 to 1913 (Toulouse 1971: 147). The remaining four are a jar, a 12 oz bottle, a 10 oz bottle embossed "SQUIRE DINGEE", and a 2 oz. bottle embossed "DR. PRICE'S DELICIOUS FLAVORING EXTRACTS". The 10-oz bottle held a sauce and dates 1873 to 1923 (Zumwalt 1980: 117).

The milk bottle is a fragment with incomplete and unidentifiable embossed lettering.

The 86 tin can fragments listed under the Miscellaneous artifact category below may represent at least one general food can.

Beef, sheep or goat, bony fish, duck, and pig are represented in the faunal remains from this level .

S2-L2

Food artifacts from this level totaled 41: 27 glass food containers, three extract bottles, two catsup bottles, two mustard bottles, five possible general food cans, and two sardine cans.

The general glass food containers, both bottles and jars, are all hand finished except one, a 4 oz. bottle with an Owens Bottle company mark on its base, 1911 to 1929 (Toulouse 1971: 393). The others ranged in capacity from 7 oz. to 32 oz. Four have "C S & Co" base mark ca. 1875 to 1913 (Toulouse 1971: 147), three have a "CB" base mark dated 1830 to ca. 1920, (Toulouse 1971: 113), and one is marked "I.G. Co." and dates ca. 1870 to 1895 (Toulouse 1971: 261). In addition to the glass containers whose specific contents are unknown are six other food bottles. Two of these are embossed "SHREWSBURY TOMATO CATSUP E.C. HAZARD & CO. NEW YORK" a product dating 1883 to ca. 1918 (Zumwalt

1980: 149). One of the extracts is embossed "J.A. FOLGER & CO. PIONEER FLAVORING EXTRACTS SAN FRANCISCO" dating from 1878 (Zumwalt 1980: 151), one has "DR. PRICE'S AMERICAN PERFUME STEELE AND PRICE" dating 1874 to ca. 1910 (Zumwalt 1980: 450), and one is marked "C.D. KNIGHT PHILa". Between 1887 and 1929 Knight produced an extract for use in cooking (Zumwalt 1980: 263). One barrel mustard, embossed "VGF", has a glass tipped pontil scar, and is undated by Zumwalt (1980: 410). The other mustard is a 5 oz. bottle embossed "CHARLES GULDEN NEW YORK" dating from ca. 1875 (Zumwalt 1980: 188).

The general food cans are listed in the Miscellaneous category because their deteriorated condition makes it impossible to know for sure that they once contained food, or some other product.

In this lens, chicken, beef, sheep or goat, bony fish, and a piece of eggshell were found. No food artifacts were found in S2-L3.

Food Preparation and Consumption

A total of 264 artifacts, or 21 percent of the total, were classified in this category (Table 3.11). These include artifacts used both in the kitchen and on the table. Several of the bowls have sooted exteriors indicating that they had been placed on top of a kitchen range.

Some of the earthenware and porcelain forms have maker's marks on them. In S1-L2 a Powell and Bishop mark and a Canonsburg mark dating 1876 to 1878 (Godden 1964: 509) and 1900 to 1978 (Kovel and Kovel 1986: 54) are on a plate with a molded wheat pattern and a plate with a floral decal and a herringbone background pattern on the rim. A bowl without a mark also has the wheat pattern and an unmarked cup, saucer, serving bowl, and individual bowl have the decal and herringbone decoration.

S2-L1 contains 10 marked forms: three Stevhenville Pottery Co. saucers, 1879 to 1960 (Lehner 1980: 144); three Furnival and Sons dinner plates, ca. 1818 to 1890 (Godden 1964: 263); a J. & G. Meakin small plate, ca. 1890 to turn-of-the-century (Godden 1964: 427); a Haviland porcelain bowl with a hand painted fruit design, ca. 1900 to present (Kovel and Kovel 1986: 230); a Thomas Hughes small plate, 1860 to 1894 (Godden 1964: 339); and a Canonsburg plate with a floral decal and herringbone background dated above. Except where mentioned, the forms are undecorated.

Seventeen forms in S2-L2 have maker's marks. These are: two W. Adams small plates, 1890 to 1896 (Godden 1964: 22); one Alfred Meakin saucer, ca. 1875-1897, and a saucer dating ca. 1891-1897 (Godden 1964: 425); a Trenton Pottery Co. plate, 1853 - ca. 1902 (Kovel and Kovel 1986: 214); a Thomas Hughes small plate dated above; two J. & G. Meakin saucers, one with molded ribs, dated above; and three saucers, an oval bowl, three small plates, a dinner plate, and a pitcher made by the Steubenville Pottery Co. dated above. The pitcher has a red brown line decal with over painted leaves and flowers. Except where mentioned, all the forms are undecorated.

Most of the other ceramic forms are plain, undecorated pieces. A few are decorated. In S1-L1 two bowls have a green transfer printed landscape decoration, a berry dish with a cream colored body has a molded rim design, and a porcelain saucer has a floral overglaze decoration.

A bowl with a transfer printed design, a porcelain saucer with a handpainted floral decoration, an unidentified form with a yellow green overall glaze, and a cup, saucer, serving bowl, and small individual bowl decorated with a gold rim line and floral decal design were found in S1-L2.

Material		Form	S1-L1	S1-L2	S2-L1	S2-L2	S2-L3	Total
Glass		Stem Ware		2	6	13	1	23
		Tumbler			15	4		19
		Mug		1				1
		Berry Dish	1		10	11		22
		Bowl	1	1	3			5
		Sugar Bowl			1			1
		Pitcher			2			2
		Pressed Glass				2		2
		Unid.				2		2
Ceramic	Hardpaste White Earthenware	Dinner Pl.		2	7	9		19
		Small Pl.			2	4		6
		Berry Dish	1					1
		Bowl	2	4	1	3		10
		Serving B.		1		1		2
		Saucer	1	2	3	7		13
		Cup		4	5	13		22
		Pitcher				1		1
		Unid.	5	3	2	3	1	14
	Porcelain	Saucer		1		1		2
		Cup				1		1
		Bowl			1			1
		Ch. Bowl				1		1
		Unid.	1	2	1			4
	Yellowware	Bowl	3	1				4
		Teapot				2		2
	Softpaste Ea.	Mexican	7	16	4	2		29
		Papago	15	10	10	15	2	52
Metal		Tsp.		1				1
		Tbsp.			1	1		2
	Wood Handle	Fork				1		1
	Bone Handle	Knife			1			1
Total			37	51	75	97	4	264

Table 3.11

Feature 10 Food Preparation and Consumption Artifacts

An unidentified form from S2-L1 has a gold rim band dating ca. 1876 to the present (Kovel and Kovel 1986: 257).

S2-L2 contained only seven forms that are decorated and unmarked. These are: a cup with a blue transfer and one with a brown transfer printed design; a dinner plate wih a decal on the rim, handpainted overglaze highlights, and gold line work; an unidentified peasant ware form with a stamped and banded decoration; a porcelain tea cup with handpainted birds on a branch; a softpaste earthenware teapot with a brown mottled glaze; and a brown glazed softpaste buff earthenware with a molded "Rebecca at the well" scene.

One of the pressed glass pieces from S2-L2 is SCA in color and dates 1880 to 1919 (Ayres 1984: 128).

Household Furnishings

Only 39 artifacts, or 3 percent of the total could be classified as household furnishings related.

S1-L1

Only a redware flower pot was found in this level.

S1-L2

Three ceramic artifacts, a hardpaste white earthenware wash basin, a procelain vase with a handpainted floral design, and a plaster figurine of unidentifiable form are from S1-L2.

S2-L1

Fourteen artifacts, seven kerosene lamp chimneys, a glass lamp globe, a possible glass vase, a redware flower pot, a hardpaste white earthenware wash basin, a brass lamp, a furniture tack, and a window shade roller bracket, came from this level.

S2-L2

Twenty artifacts are from this level: 13 kerosene lamp chimneys, a lamp globe, a lamp shade, a vase with a glass tipped pontil scar, a hardpaste white earthenware chamber pot lid and wash basin, and two kerosene lamp wick assemblies.

S2-L3

Only a kerosene lamp chimney was found in this level.

Household Maintenance

Only six artifacts are classified in this category, three 2 oz. sewing machine oil bottles, one of which is labled "...Se... Machine ..." (S2-L1) and three 2 oz. glue bottles (S2-L2) all of which are 2 oz. cone shaped bottles having daubers with metal stems.

Architecture

Artifacts related to architecture number 28, or two percent of the total.

S1-L1

This level contained an electric light bulb and a fired adobe brick.

S1-L2

An electric light bulb, a fired adobe brick, and a piece of electrical wiring were found in S1-L2.

S2-L1

S2-L1 produced an electric light bulb, five panes of window glass, a ceramic electric fuse, and a metal electrical fixture.

S2-L2

Fifteen artifacts, including 12 panes of window glass, a fired adobe brick, a door knob with a metal shank, and a house door key, were found in this level.

The estimated number of panes of window glass represented is based on the occurrence of fragments of this glass in 14 different bags of artifacts from S2-L1 and S2-L2. Probably the five panes in S2-L1 and the 12 panes of S2-L2 actually represent no more than a total of five panes based on color and thickness.

Leisure and Recreation

In this category are 88 artifacts representing seven percent of the total encompassing four distinct categories: soda, alcoholic beverages, toys, and firearms (Table 3.12).

The soda bottle (S2-L1), embossed "Crystal Bottling Works Tucson, Arizona", dates ca. 1908 to 1934 (Kimball 1908: 97; Arizona Directory Co. 1934: 189).

With three exceptions, all of the 37 alcoholic beverage bottles are hand finished. These three are all machine made beer bottles with crown finishes, one from S1-L1 and two from S2-L1. One of the latter was made by William Franzen and Sons, sometime between 1903 and 1929 (Toulouse 1971: 536).

From S2-L1 came a whiskey bottle with "San Francisco" embossed on it and a beer bottle made by the Frederick Hampson Glass Works, ca. 1880-1900 (Toulouse 1971: 202).

In S2-L2 only two beer bottles have maker's marks, one of A. and D. H. Chambers, ca. 1880-1910 and one of the Frederick Hampson Glass Works ca. 1880-1900 (Toulouse 1971: 38, 202).

The 19 wine or champagne bottles are invariably shades of green, some have deep kickups, and all are hand finished.

Artifact	Class		S1-L1	S1-L2	S2-L1	S2-L2	S2-L3	Total
Soda		Bottle			1			1
Alcohol Bev.	Beer	Bottle	3	1	4	6	1	15
	Wine/Ch.	Bottle	3	1	1	14		19
	Whiskey	Bottle			1			1
	Sample Whiskey	Bottle			1			1
	Unident. Liquor	Bottle				1		1
Toys	Marble		1					1
	Jack				1			1
	Harmonica				2			2
	Doll				1	1		2
	Doll Part				2	13	2	17
	Dish					1		1
	Cup				1	6		7
	Mex. Plate					1		1
	Plate					1		1
	Chamber Pot					1		1
	Saucer					4		4
	Teapot Lid					2		2
	Thimble					1		1
	Revolver					2		2
	Cartridge					7		7
Totals			7	2	15	61	3	88

Table 3.12
Feature 10 Leisure and Recreation Artifacts

The sample whiskey bottle, made in the same way as full sized bottles, holds 1 oz.

With the possible exception of the limestone marble and the harmonicas, the toys are those of a female. Among these are two dolls and 17 doll parts, all from Stratum 2. The two dolls are incomplete solid, molded "Frozen Charlotte" types dating to the 1850s to ca. 1880 (Pritchett and Pastron 1983: 327, 330).

The parts include heads (7), legs (4), arms (4), and bodies (2) from small solid dolls, legs and arms that had originally been attached to small cloth bodies, and head and shoulder fragments from large dolls having cloth bodies. All are porcelain and most have a clear glaze applied. A few are unglazed. Some have shoes, usually hand painted black (one was gold), and hair is usually painted black (one is blond).

Table 3.14 indicates the variety of toy dishes found in Feature 10. These, like the dolls, all came from Stratum 2, all are made of porcelain with a clear glaze, and many are complete. The most numerous form is the cup. All but two of these are undecorated. Both are from S2-L2 and have a handpainted, polychrome floral design with gold embellishments.

The Mexican made plate is a clear glazed redware with daubs of white and molded floral and geometric design on the rim. It is 1 3/8 in. in diameter.

Only three of the remaining ceramic forms have decorative elements. The four saucers and the teapot lid have a gold design, and the dish is a 3 1/2 in. square form with a molted cat's face. One of the saucers is 2 5/16 in. and two are 3 in., in diameter. In addition to gold, the teapot has a handpainted pink, blue, and red floral decoration on it.

The thimble is a child-sized object that may not be a toy; it is functional for a small finger whether that of an adult or child. Other metal forms found are a jack and two harmonicas.

Nine firearms related artifacts were found in S2-L2. These are two revolvers and seven cartridges. One of the revolvers is in very poor condition. It was found without a barrel but did have traces of a wooden grip. Given its condition, any marks or its caliber could not be identified. A .22 caliber revolver with a bird head grip dating 1871-1879 (Flayderman 1983: 262) also was found. This weapon, which was made by the Whitney Arms Co., had no barrel when found. The cartridges consist of six fired .22 caliber short cases and a badly corroded complete, possible .38 caliber, case. The .22 caliber short dates 1857 to the present and the .38 caliber possibly 1877 to the present (Barnes 1972: 273, 162-163).

Medical and Health

In Feature 10, 145 medical and health related artifacts were recovered (Table 3.13). Of these, 44 are embossed and unembossed proprietary medicine bottles and jars, 93 are prescription ware bottles, five are homeopathic vials, and three are miscellaneous.

All of the containers are hand finished except where noted. In general, the proprietary containers are green, aqua, brown, or occasionally clear in color, and the prescription ware is clear. A wide range of shapes and sizes are present in both types. Round, square, and rectangular shapes are the most common. Sizes range from one-half ounce to 16 oz. with 2 oz. to 8 oz. being the most common.

In S1-L1 was a Vaseline jar, a "The Celebrated HHH Horse Medicine" bottle, and three prescription ware bottles of 1/4, 1, and 4 oz. capacity. The 1 oz. bottle has "I.G. Co." the mark of the Ihmsen Glass Co. on its base, ca. 1870 to 1895 (Toulouse 1971: 261). The HHH bottle dates ca. 1868 to 1915 (Wilson and Wilson 1971: 23; Herskovitz 1978: 16; Devner 1968: 44). The Vaseline jar dates 1870 to ca. 1950 (Brand Name Foundation 1947: np; Wilson and Wilson 1971: 110).

Three proprietary containers were found in S1-L2. One of these was a machine made Vaseline jar dating 1903 to 1950 (Brand Name Foundation 1947: np; Wilson and Wilson 1971: 110) one was a machine made bottle with the I in a diamond mark of the Illinois Glass Co. on its base, 1916-1929 (Toulouse 1971: 264), and one was unembossed.

S2-L1 produced 22 proprietary and prescription containers. Five of the proprietary bottles are unembossed, one of these is machine made (1903-present) and one has the unidentified mark "I.C.G. Co." on its base. Five are Vaseline jars dated as above, and one is embossed, "DR. KENNDY'S MEDICAL DISCOVERY ROXBURY, MASS."

The prescription ware bottles are unembossed except a few have a base mark. These include an "S" in a diamond (unidentified) and two McC's, 1832 to ca. 1886 (Toulouse 1971: 351).

Slightly over 75 percent (109) of the artifacts in the medical and health function category came from S2-L2. None of the 77 prescription ware bottles is embossed except for a few base marks. There are three McC (dated above) and six I.G. Co. (dated above) marks that are dated. Three "H", a "CW", a "B.B. Co", and a B in a circle are unidentified. One bottle has a four leaf clover on its base.

Nine of the 28 proprietary containers are unembossed. Embossed bottles and jars are: three Vaseline jars; two "AYER'S CHERRY PECTORAL LOWELL, MASS."; two AYER'S COMPOUND EXTRACT SARSAPARILLA LOWELL, MASS."; one "DR. D. JAYNE'S LINIMENT COUNTER IRRITANT PHILADA"; one AYRE'S PILLS LOWELL, MASS."; one base, "BREMEN H. HEYE HAMBURG"; one "Lysol" with an O in a square, 1911 to 1929 (Toulouse 1971: 393); one "DR. KINGS' DISCOVERY H.E. BUCKLEN AND CO." 1880 to ?, (Fike 1987: 33); one "AINAXAB THE CELEBRATED EGYPTIAN ELIXIR FOR THE SKIN A.J. GIRARDIN AND CO. SAN FRANCISCO"; and five "SYRUP OF FIGS CALIFORNIA FIG SYRUP CO. SAN FRANCISCO, CAL."

Artifact	Class	S1-L1	S1-L2	S2-L1	S2-L2	S2-L3	Totals
	Proprietary Medicine	2	3	11	29		44
	Prescription Ware	3		11	77	2	93
	Homeopathic Vial			2	3		5
	Hot Water Bottle Stopper		1				1
	Eyedropper			1			1
	Syringe with Plunger				1		1
	Totals	5	4	25	109	2	145

Table 3.13

Feature 10 Medical and Health Artifacts

The Vaseline jars date 1870 - 1950 (Brand Names Foundation 1947: np; Wilson and Wilson 1971: 110). Dr. Pitchers' Castoria dates 1868 to ca. 1920 based on the patent date, and the Jaynes product dates 1830-1950 (Brand Names Foundation 1947: np).

Personal

In Feature 10, 218 artifacts of a personal nature were found (Table 3.14). On a functional basis, 46 are related to personal care, 159 are clothing and personal adornment artifacts, three are religious, and 10 are miscellaneous. Nearly 73 percent of these were clothing and adornment related artifacts.

Only one personal artifact each came from S1-L1 and S2-L3. In the former is a plastic watch strap and in the latter is a child's shoe.

From S2-L1 are 69 artifacts, most of which are clothing related. In this level were found the rosary, crucifix, and medal. These are probably all part of the same rosary.

S2-L2 produced nearly 67 percent (145) of the total artifacts in this category.

The personal artifacts from Feature 10 reflect the presence of men, women, and children. The collar buttons and pocket knife are male artifacts. Women are represented by the perfume or toilet water bottles, cosmetic containers, Florida water bottles, the barrette, the corset parts, the rubber douche set, and the fan. Children's artifacts include the slate boards and pencils and the child's shoe.

Four of the toothpowder bottles are embossed "RUBIFOAM FOR THE TEETH PUT UP BY E.W. HOYT & CO. LOWELL, MASS." and one is labelled "...THE TEETH...BREATH." The latter from S2-L2 is Sozodent a tooth cleaning preparation. Rubifoam dates ca. 1875 to about 1915 (Devner 1970: 55). One of the S2-L2 bottles is labeled

"COLGATE & CO. PE...RS NEW YORK". This was tentatively classified as a toothpowder bottle dating 1806 to 1920 (Periodical Publishers Assoc. 1934: 81).

	Artifact Class	S1-L1	S1-L2	S2-L1	S2-L2	S2-L3	Totals
Glass	Toothpaste			3	3		6
	Perfume & Toilet Water		1	1	2		4
	Cosmetics			1	2		3
	Deodorant			1			1
	Florida Water				4		4
	Shoe Polish			4	11		15
	Button			22	49		71
	Rosary			1			1
	Hand Mirror				1		1
	Barrette				1		1
	Clothing Buckle				1		1
	Clothing Buckle			3			3
	Corset			2	2		4
	Collar Button			1			1
Metal	Shoe Eyelet			6	17		23
	Shoe Hook				3		3
	Hook Eye				1		1
	Button				2		2
Other	Pocket Knife				1		1
	Coin Purse			1	1		2
	Crucifix			1			1
	Religious Medal			1			1
	Bone Button			6	2		8
	Bone Collar Button				1		1
	Bone Fan			1			1
	Shell Button			8	24		32
	School Slate		1	1	2		4
	Slate Pencil				2		2
	Hard Rubber Comb			3	3		6
	Hard Rubber Belt Link				1		1
	Shoe				5		5
	Child's Shoe					1	1
	Brush				1		1
	Bone Toothbrush				1		1
	Plastic Watch Strap	1					1
	Rubber Douche Set			2	2		4
Total		1	2	69	145	1	218

Table 3.14
Feature 10 Personal Artifacts

The milk glass deodorant container is embossed "MUM MFG. CO. PHILA. PA." This product dates 1888 to 1950 (Periodical Publishers Assoc. 1934: 18).

The four Florida water bottles have "FLORIDA WATER MURRAY & LANMAN DRUGGISTS NEW YORK" on them.

Only the S2-L1 shoe polish bottles labeled "WHITTEMORE BOSTON U.S.A." are embossed. The other bottles in the personal category are unmarked.

Two of the hard rubber combs, one each from S2-L1 and S2-L2 have impressed marks. The former has "OLIVE DORE WARRANTED UNBREAKABLE 89" adjacent to a figure of a man sawing a log with a comb and the latter has "...COMB CO. GOODYEAR" on it.

Transportation

Only two transportation related artifacts were recovered from Feature 10, a horseshoe and a bicycle sprocket, both from S2-L2.

Tools and Hardware

The Tools and Hardware category includes a large percentage of the Feature 10 artifacts (239) but most (93 percent) are square cut, wire, and unidentified nails (Table 3.17). The remaining artifacts are a miscellaneous collection of wire, bolts, copper tubing, iron fragments, a washer, a spring hinge, and screen door hook. The Tools and Hardware artifacts were more or less evenly scattered throughout first four levels, but Stratum 2 had more than Stratum 1. The square cut nails generally date 1860-1900 and wire nails 1890 to present.

Artifact Class	Type	S1-L1	S1-L2	S2-L1	S1-L2	Totals
Nail	Unident.	13	43		33	89
	Square Cut		5	35	2	42
	Wire	40	2	46	2	90
	9d Finishing	1				1
Wire	Iron			1	1	2
	Copper		1	2	1	4
Tubing	Copper				4	4
Strap	Iron	1				1
Angle Iron		1				1
Hook	Screen Door			1		1
Washer	Iron			1		1
Hinge	Spring			1		1
Bolt	Carriage			1		1
	Machine			1		1
Totals		56	51	89	43	239

Table 3.15

Feature 10 Tools and Hardware

Communications

Eight artifacts are classified as communications related. These are a glass ink well and two whole glass ink bottles from S2-L1, and three whole glass ink bottles, a ceramic ink bottle, and a graphite stick from a pencil from S2-L2. The ink well and three of the ink bottles are embossed "CARTERS", one ink bottle has "CARTER'S INDELIBLE INK" on it, and one has "L.H. THOMAS" on it. All are handfinished.

Miscellaneous

Thirty artifacts were classified as Miscellaneous and were found in the upper four levels. Tin cans are discussed under food because it is likely they were food containers. From S1-L1 are a pitchfork, a carbon battery core, and two prehistoric flakes. Six prehistoric flakes were found in S1-L2 and S2-L1 produced 10 unidentified burned seeds, a prehistoric point, and a Anomia sp. shell from the Pacific Ocean. The point may be an early man or archaic point that broke and was heavily reworked.

A bottle once containing turpentine, two coins (one of which has "Republica Peruana 186?" on it,) a whiskbroom top cap, a graphite stick from a carpenter's pencil, two cloth fragments, and a Pacific Ocean shell, Chione sp. came from S2-L2

Unidentified

One hundred one artifacts could not be assigned to a functional category frequently because they were too fragmentary These represent eight percent of the total minimum number of artifacts from Feature 10 and are classified as unidentified. Pieces of SCA glass in S1-L2 and S2-L2 date 1880-1919 (Ayres 1984: 128) . An I in a diamond bottle base mark in S2-L1 dates 1916-1929 (Toulouse 1971: 264). An Owens made bottle in S2-L1 dates 1911 to 1929 (Toulouse 1971: 393). Plastic fragments were found in S1-L1.

Feature 10 Summary

Feature 10 is a relatively shallow, trash-filled privy pit associated with the house on Lot 6. It also may have been used by the residents of the dwelling on Lot 17, although there is no evidence to support this statement, except the proximity of the two houses and the fact that no privy is shown on Lot 17 on the Sanborn maps.

Artifacts related to women and children are numerous in Feature 10. These were found in all levels but the majority, 68 percent, were in S2-L2 (Table 3.14).

Except for the marble and the harmonicas, probably all boy's toys, the majority of the toys are toy dishes and dolls used by one or more girls. Surprisingly many of the toy dishes are complete. Why these were thrown into a privy remains a mystery.

Women's artifacts include personal care items, clothing parts, a hand mirror, and a fan (Table 3.14) for a total of 20. S2-L1 and S2-L2 produced 31 pieces of corsets. Because of the way in which these were recorded they are listed in Table 3.16 as two corsets - for each level is actually present. The same is true for the douche sets. Actually parts of what appear to be two different sets (based on the color of the rubber tubing) were found, one in each level, S2-L1 and S2-L2 (Table 3.14).

These artifacts suggest that Feature 10 was used by a family, including at least one female child and possibly with one male child. The food, food preparation and consumption, and household furnishings artifacts along with the other leisure and recreation and personal artifacts all support the idea that Feature 10 material culture was family -generated.

Dating

Artifact dates (Fig. 3.7) and Sanborn map data provide a consistent picture of the age of this feature.   The privy was shown on the 1896 Sanborn map but not on the preceding map (1889) or on the

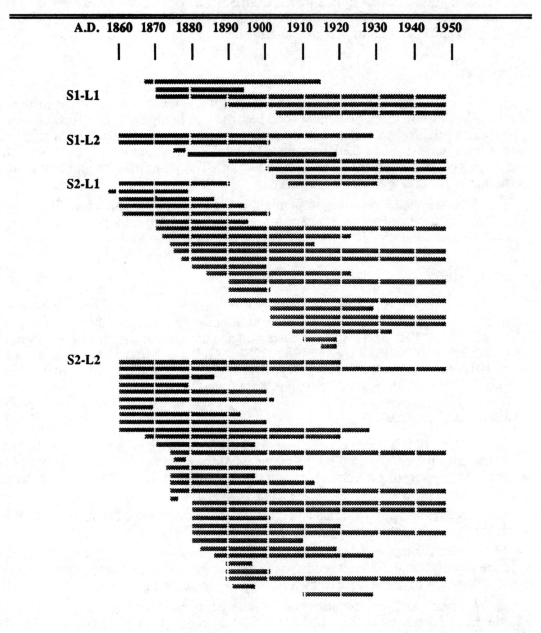

Figure 3.7
Feature 10 Artifact Date Ranges

following one (1901). Although the Sanborn maps did not always illustrate every outbuilding present, the fact that this one was shown only in 1896 suggests that it might have been abandoned after its first filling. Abandonment would have required moving the privy building to a new location or the installation of plumbing in the house. The former is more likely but none show on the later Sanborn maps. Commonly, Tucson privies were cleaned out when they became full, thus making them available for reuse.

As a group the artifacts neatly bracket the 1896 date (Fig. 3.7). With a few exceptions explained below, all of the artifacts can be accounted for within a range of six years, 1894 to 1900. At any rate, the use of the latrine probably did not date later than 1900 because if it did, it most likely would have been shown on Sanborn's 1901 edition of its maps.

Six artifacts had end dates earlier than 1894. In S1-L2 was a plate dating 1876 to 1878. From S2-L1 was a McCully-made beer bottle (1832 to 1886, actually ca. 1873 to 1886), a frozen Charlotte doll (1850 to ca. 1880), and a dinner plate (1818 to 1890). A coin dating to the 1860s and a pistol made between 1871 and 1879 came from S2-L2. One commonly finds artifacts such as these in proveniences originating at a later date. All are types of artifacts that had the potential for use for years after their period of manufacture. Bottles normally have a short period between the dates of manufacture, use, and discard, but beer bottles of this era were frequently reused and this specimen could have been as well. It is not uncommon in Arizona to find beer bottles that predate the proveniences in which they are found. Some of the lag may be a result of incorrect dates in Toulouse (1971).

All of the levels except S2-L3 had one or more artifacts with beginning dates postdating 1900. Most, if not all, of these probably were artifacts deposited in the two intrusive pits that were found to extend into S2-L1.

In S1-L1 was a machine made bottle (1903 to the present) and in S1-L2 was a machine made bottle and one with an Illinois Glass Company mark (1916-1929). In addition to an example each of the artifacts in S1-L2, S2-L1 had an Owens Bottle Company bottle (1911 to 1929), a machine made "WF&S" beer bottle (1903 to 1929), and a soda bottle (1908 to 1934). S2-L2 had two Owens Bottle Company bottles. It is likely that the bottles in S2-L2 came from the intrusive pit and had not been part of the original S2-L2 deposit.

Given the dates of these artifacts, it appears that the trash in the intrusive pits was deposited sometime between 1916 and 1929.

Lot 7

Lot 7 features are shown here in Figure 3.8 and also on Figures 1.2 and 1.3.

Feature 4

Feature 4 is the first of the features recovered from Lot 7 to be discussed here (Fig. 3.8). This large, circular pit was located in backhoe Trench 6. This trench cut through its west side during testing, leaving a portion of the pit on the west side of the backhoe trench. Most of the pit was left undisturbed on the east side of the trench.

Feature 4 is similar in form to those identified as features 5, 15, and 17. It is located in Lot 7 in what was once the backyard of 313, later 315, South Main Street. The pit, which was cut into solid caliche, was about 7 ft. in diameter at the top and widened to 7 ft. 8 in. at the base. It was 4 ft. 2 in. in depth and had a flat, smooth floor.

Over the top of the pit was an 8 in. thick layer of sheet trash labeled S1-L1 (Fig.3.9). This sheet trash was found across much of the site. Its upper parts were undoubtedly disturbed by demolition and construction activities on the block. The level was a loosely compacted dark brownish grey sandy silt containing ash, charcoal, and numerous artifacts. Above this was a sterile layer of redeposited caliche and soil underlying the parking lot paving. This redeposited layer was about 12 in. thick and was placed there during the construction of the Convention Center and the parking lot. That part of it over the feature was removed by backhoe.

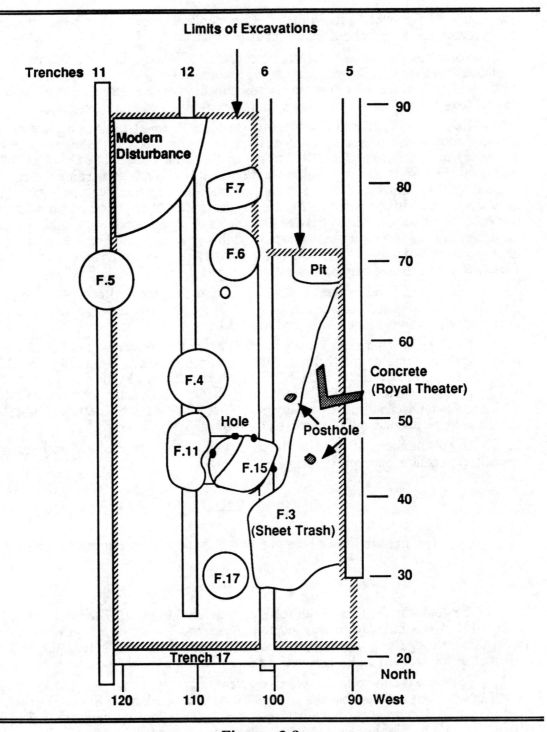

Figure 3.8
Lot 7 Archaeological Features

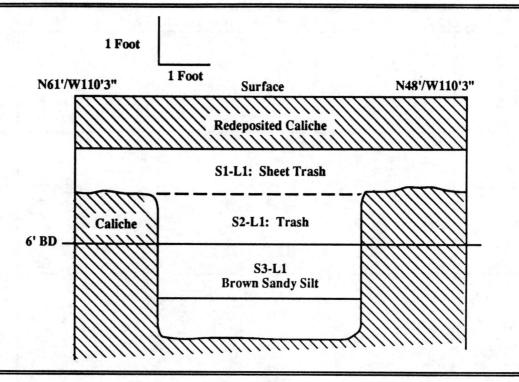

Figure 3.9
Feature 4 Profile

The contents of the pit were divided into two strata, a 3 in. thick ash lens on top and the fill below it. The ash lens contained numerous artifacts and appears to have been the final deposit thrown into the pit. The fill below the lens was 3 ft. 11 in. thick and was generally a homogeneous, loosely compacted bown sandy silt with artifacts, ash and charcoal, and organic stains.

Two small holes, one 5 in. and one 4 in. in diameter, were found in the pit wall 7 in. above the floor. The larger of the two was directed to the east and the other was angled to the northwest These holes are similar to those found in features 5, 15, and 17.

Artifacts

Collected from Feature 4 were 631 whole artifact fragments representing a minimum of 202 individual objects (Table 3.16).

Food

No food related artifacts were found in Feature 4, although the tin cans listed in the Miscellaneous category may have been food containers.

Food Preparation and Consumption

Seventeen percent of the total, or 35 artifacts, were placed in this category (Table 3.17). These include glass and ceramic artifacts used both for food preparation (in the kitchen) and consumption (on the table).

	FP&C	HF	Arch.	L&R	M&H	Pers.	Trans.	T&H	Misc.	Unid.	Total
S1-L1											
Glass	2	1	1	4	5					2	15
Ceramic	11		3								14
Metal		1	1	3			1	10	2	5	23
Other						8			6		14
Total	13	2	5	7	5	8	1	10	8	7	66
S2-L1											
Glass				3	2	3				2	10
Ceramic	6		3								9
Metal		2				1			12	2	17
Other										10	10
Total	6	2	3	3	2	4	0	12	12	2	46
S2-L1											
Glass	37	9	28	6	8	33				22	158
Ceramic	36	2		1	4						43
Metal	1	3		1	3	15		89		12	124
Other	1					21			12	7	41
Total	75	14	28	8	15	69	0	89	12	41	366
S3-L1											
Glass	1		1	2						2	6
Ceramic	7										7
Metal			1					23	1	1	26
Other						1			24		25
Total	8	0	1	3	0	1	0	23	25	3	64
S3-L2											
Glass		1	1	2						2	6
Ceramic	8										8
Metal								9	1		10
Other										1	1
Total	8	1	1	2	0	0	0	9	1	3	25
Total	35	5	10	5	7	13	1	54	46	16	202

Table 3.16
Feature 4 Artifacts by Function

Included in the assemblage from Feature 4 are three Mexican and 20 Papago forms. Two Papago bowls (S3-L1) are of unslipped brown ware with a dark carbon streak. All three have sooted bases indicating their use for cooking purposes.

None of the earthenwares or procelain forms have maker's marks. A pitcher and an unidentified porcelain form have gold rim bands, which according to Kovel and Kovel (1986: 257), postdate 1876. One of the tumblers has turned pink in color and dates ca. 1919 to 1940s (see Feature 2 discussion).

Household Furnishings

Five artifacts were identified as furnishings. These are a kerosene lamp chimney and a furniture tack from S1-L1, a kerosene lamp font and a lamp wick assembly from S2-L1, and a kerosene lamp chimney from S3-L2.

Material		Form	S1-L1	S2-L1	S3-L1	S3-L2	Total
Glass		Stemware			1		1
		Tumbler	2				2
Ceramic	Hardpaste White Earthenware	Small Plate	1				1
		Serving Bowl			1		1
		Bowl		1			1
		Saucer			1		1
		Unid.	1			1	2
	Porcelain	Pitcher	1	1			2
		Unid.	1				1
	Softpaste Earthenware	Mexican Forms	3				3
		Papago Forms	5	4	5	6	20
Totals			13	6	8	8	35

Table 3.17
Feature 4 Food Preparation and Consumption Artifacts

Architecture

The architectural artifacts number 10, including window glass from S1-L1, S3-L1, and S3-L2; six small fired adobe bricks from S1-L1 (3) and S2-L1 (3); and a rim knob lock from S1-L1.

The bricks are red-orange in color, are irregular in form, and are often slightly concave on one surface. They range from 1.5 to 2 in. in thickness, 3.5 to 3.75 in width, and 7.0 to 7.5 in length. They were loose in the fill above and on top of the pit in Feature 4 and were not part of a lining for the pit.

Leisure and Recreation

In this category are three beer bottles, one wine bottle, and three cartridges from S1-L1; two soda bottles and one beer bottle from S2-L1; two wine bottles and one cartridge from S3-L1; and one beer bottle and one pernod bottle from S3-L2. The pernod bottle was embossed,

"BD PERNOD COUVET." None of the other bottles displayed legible marks. The beer bottles are of a type in use from about 1880 to 1910.

The two soda bottles have Hutchinson stoppers and are embossed "HERVE & CARBON J.F.I. TUCSON". The stopper dates 1879 to 1912 (Holscher 1965: 34-35) . The dates for J.F.I. are unknown.

The four cartridges were a .56-56 Spencer rim fire, 1862-1920 (Barnes 1972: 281) and two .44-40, 1873-1942 (Barnes 1972: 61) from S1-L1, and a .41 caliber cartridge from S3-L1 dating 1877-1930 (Barnes 1972: 165).

Medical and Health

In this category are five prescription bottles from S1-L1 (4) and S2-L1 (1), and two proprietary medicine bottles, one each from the same proviences. None of these bottles have legible labels.

Personal

Thirteen personal artifacts, eight shell buttons (S1-L1), three glass and one metal buttons (S2-L1), and one shell button (S3-L1) were recovered from Feature 4.

Transportation

Only one artifact related to transportation, a bit from a horse bridle, was identified.

Tools and Hardware

Most of the artifacts in this category are nails, both square cut (40) and wire (11). In addition, a bolt, a washer, and a hammer head were found (Table 3.18).

Artifact Class	Type	S1-L1	S1-L2	S2-L1	S1-L2	Totals
Nail	Square Cut	10				40
	Wire			11		11
Bolt			1			1
Washer				1		1
Hammer				1		1
Totals		10	12	23	9	54

Table 3.18
Feature 4 Tools and Hardware

Miscellaneous

Miscellaneous artifacts totaled 46 (Table 3.19) and include four tin cans, possibly food cans, and six seashells. The shells are a Trachycardium panamense, a pitar sp., an Arca mutabilis, a Hipponin sp., one from the Tellin family, and one unidentified.

The presence of Gulf of California shell is not unexpected in urban Tucson trash deposits. In the case of Feature 4 more than usual were found, all were in the ash lens, S2-L1. These may have been part of a personal collection. None are from edible species.

	Luggage	Tin Can	Bucket	Lead/Ore	Copper / Ore	Flake	Mano	Shell	Totals
S1 - L1	1	1		1		5			8
S2 - L2		1	1			3	1	6	12
S3 - L1					5	19			25
S3 - L2		1						1	
Totals	1	4	1	1	5	27	1	6	46

Table 3.19
Feature 4 Miscellaneous Artifacts

Unidentified

The Feature 4 assemblage includes 16 artifacts whose form and function could not be determined.

Summary Feature 4

The circular, vertically sided, flat floored pit labelled Feature 4 is, like its three relatives on Lot 7, of unknown function. Further discussion of these features can be found below. Like the others, Feature 4 has the ubiquitous and enigmatic holes in the wall.

There appears to be three depositional events represented in Feature 4, the pit fill itself (S3-L1 and L2), the ash lens (S2-L1) at the top of the pit, and the sheet trash layer (S1-L1) over these. The sheet trash should have no connection with the pit fill, and should postdate it and the ash lens. The ash lens should also postdate the pit fill.

Forty-four percent (89) of the artifacts came from S1-L1 and 23 percent came from S2-L1. Relatively few artifacts (33 percent) were found in the pit fill below the ash lens. This fact, plus the homogeneity of the fill, may indicate that the pit was filled over a short time rather than filling slowing as trash gradually accumulated in it.

In a general way the artifacts in all the Feature 4 levels tend to be very similar. For example, kerosene lamp parts, Papago ceramics, and alcoholic beverage bottles were recovered from each of the four levels.

Mexican made ceramics came only from S1-L1 and Papago bowls used for cooking purposes were found only in Stratum 3, that is in the pit.

With the possible exception of the tin cans found in every level, no food artifacts were noted.

Artifacts relating specifically to women and children, always in the minority in Tucson's urban trash deposits, were nonexistent.

In general, the trash in Feature 4 appears to have originated from one or more Mexican families, but evidence to support that suggestion is meager at best.

Dating

As mentioned above, the three strata should date progressively earlier as we proceed downward. However, the paucity of datable artifacts from the feature hampers the process of assigning reliable dates to each level (Fig. 3.10). With the exception of the square cut nail date (1860 to 1900), one can account for all of the datable artifacts in S1-L1 with a range of 1910 to

1920. In a context such as Feature 4, square cut nails are of little value in establishing feature dates. All that can be said for S2-L1, the ash lens, is that it predates 1912. As far as dates for Stratum 3 are concerned, it is safe only to suggest that the trash in it predates 1910. Possibly strata 2 and 3 are contemporary deposits.

Feature 5

Feature 5 was bisected during testing by backhoe Trench 11. The larger part of this circular, nearly vertically sided pit was located on the east side of the trench. The bottom of the backhoe trench was below the southward sloping, flat floor of the pit (Fig. 3.11).

The feature was located in the rear of the house on the west side of Lot 7.

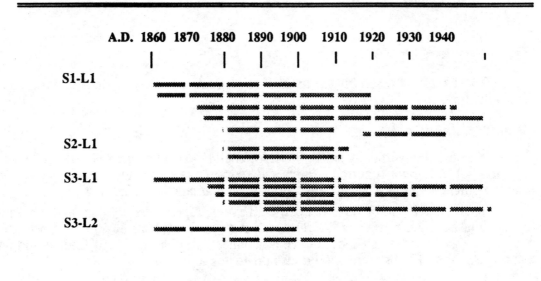

Figure 3.10
Feature 4 Artifact Date Ranges

Overlying the feature was a 10 in. layer of redeposited caliche and soil excavated during the construction of the Convention Center and placed in this area to level it and to provide a compact surface on which to put the parking lot paving. This caliche layer was removed with the backhoe and, as was the case elsewhere on lots 6, 7, and 17, it contained no artifacts.

Under the redeposited material was an 11 in. deep layer of brown sandy silt containing ash, charcoal, and numerous artifacts (Fig. 3.11). This level, designated S1-L1, was partially above, and partially in, the pit. The 2 in. to 4 in. above the top of the pit was part of the general sheet trash layer situated across these lots, the remainder was pit fill. Overall the depth of the sheet trash at this point varies considerably because it overlies the uneven surface of the solid bed of caliche found throughout the area. On the north side of Feature 5 the sheet trash was only 4 in. thick, but on the south side it was 17 in. thick. The feature cut through some of the sheet trash and was in turn covered by other sheet trash after the pit was filled. In addition, the upper part of this level was disturbed by demolition and construction activities.

The top of the feature appears to have been about 12 in. to 14 in. below the top of the redeposited caliche even though the caliche "hardpan" was below this level on the south side. This is demonstrated by the fact that on the south side of the pit, sloping trash lenses originate at that depth. Because these lenses slope downward from the south side, the pit was clearly filled from that direction possibly over a relatively long period of time.

Intruding into the bottom of S1-L1 was a 10 in. wide electric cable trench that ran approximately northeast to southwest through the middle of the feature. Although the sides of this trench were not visible 7 in. above its base, it was undoubtedly dug through the redeposied caliche and S1-L1 to provide electricity to the parking lot lighting fixtures. It was excavated sometime during the final phases of parking lot construction. The artifacts found in the trench were separated from the rest of the S1-L1 material culture as were a few artifacts collected during the testing phase backhoe work.

Running from east to west through the feature was what appeared to be an earlier, 12 in. wide trench. This trench, which was of unknown purpose, was actually cut through by Feature 5 because no trace of it could be found in the pit fill. The bottom of this trench was from 13 in. (on the east side) to 19 in. (on the west side) above the floor of Feature 5. The top of this trench was observed as high as the top of S1-L2.

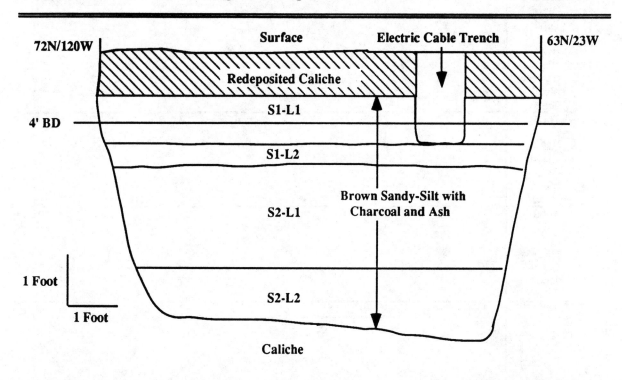

Figure 3.11
Feature 5 Profile

S1-L2, below S1-L1, was an 8 in. layer of brown sandy silt with large quantities of ash and charcoal intermixed. It was not appreciably different in character than S1-L1 but it had not been disturbed during construction.

The lower two levels S2-L1 and S2-L2 were similar in color and texture to the Stratum 1 levels. At the base of S2-L2, on the floor, was a thin layer of clay and fine silt which may have been water deposited. The floor sloped slightly to the south.

An 8 in. diameter hole was found at floor level on the south side of the pit. This was similar to those found in features 4, 15, and 17.

The top of the feature was 7.5 ft. in diameter and about 6 ft. in diameter at the base.

Artifacts

A total of 898 whole and fragmentary artifacts representing a minimum of 294 individual objects (Table 3.20) were obtained from the excavation of Feature 5. These include 21 artifacts from the backhoe trench that located the feature and from an electrical cable trench that disturbed its upper fill.

	Food	FP&C	Arch.	L&R	M&H	Personal	Trans.	T&H	Misc.	Unid.	Totals
Trench											
Glass				6	1					2	9
Ceramic		9	1								10
Metal						1		1			2
Other											0
Total		9	1	6	1	1	0	1		2	21
S1-L1											
Glass	4		2	6	1	3				4	20
Ceramic		17	1							1	19
Metal			2			1		18	1	3	25
Other				1		1			1	1	4
Total	4	17	3	9	1	5	0	18	2	9	68
S1-L2											
Glass	1	2	6	5		4				7	25
Ceramic		25									25
Metal			2					33	3	4	42
Other						1			10		11
Total	1	27	6	7	0	5	0	33	13	11	103
S2-L1											
Glass	1	4	3	9		1				5	23
Ceramic		19	1	1							21
Metal							1	17	4	6	28
Other		1				5			4	2	12
Total	1	24	4	10	0	6	1	17	8	13	94
S2-L2											
Glass		1	2			2				5	10
Ceramic											0
Metal								4	1		5
Other									3		3
Total	0	1	2	0	0	2	0	4	4	5	18
TOTALS	6	70	16	32	2	19	1	73	27	40	294

Table 3.20

Feature 5 Artifacts by Function

Food

Food related artifacts found in Feature 5 are a turned pink milk bottle dating ca. 1919 to the 1940s (see discussion in Feature 2), a machine made fruit jar, an olive oil bottle, and a sauce bottle from S1-L1; a catsup bottle from S1-L2; and a mustard bottle from S2-L1. The sauce bottle is a Lea and Perrins Worcestershire sauce, 1877-1920 (Zumwalt 1980: 269) and the catsup is embossed "TROPHY CATSUP CHICAGO PRESERVING WORKS", ca. 1883-1887 (Zumwalt 1980: 80-81).

The faunal remains make up a substantial part of the food related artifacts in Feature 5. Unfortunately only part of the bone from one level, S2-L2, was identified and analyzed (Table 3.21).

There are 140 pieces of food related faunal remains in the sample studied. Of these 132, or 94 percent, are beef bones. Included in this collection are 22 foot bones. The meat on these bones was undoubtedly used for making menudo. Other beef butchering units include the neck, chuck, ribs, loin, rump, round, and hindshank. These appear to be parts of at least 12 individual animals. The units represent both the inexpensive and the more expensive cuts of meat.

The butchering unit from the pig was the ham and from the sheep was the leg. Five bones could only be identified as either sheep or goat. These bones are from leg butchering units representing two individuals. The pig innominate was sawn as were the sheep femur and the sheep or goat femur.

Wild game is represented by an Odocoileus sp. humerus which was sawn.

It is likely that most of the 106 bones listed in Table 3.25 as small to large mammals and as unidentified also are from beef and other food related animals. At least 56 bones in these categories show evidence of butchering.

None of the S2-L2 faunal remains were burned.

Species	Minimum No. of Individuals	Number of Bones
Bos Taurus (Beef)	12	132
Odocoileus sp. (Deer)	1	1
Sus scrofa (Pig)	1	1
Ovis cf aires (Sheep)	1	2
Ovis/Capra (Sheep or Goat)	2	4
Total		140
Others		
Small to Large Mammals		106
Unidentified		19
Total		125
TOTAL		265

Table 3.21
Feature 5 Faunal Remains

Food Preparation and Consumption

Table 3.22 lists the artifacts that once had table and kitchen use.

Eight Mexican and 26 Papago ceramic forms are included in this category. Six bowls, one Mexican and five Papago, have sooted exteriors indicating their use for cooking purposes (Tables 2.20 and 2.21). The Mexican bowl is a floral decorated, green interior glazed form from the backhoe trench, as is a Papago plain brown bowl. S1-L2 produced two Papago bowls, one with, and one without, a dark core. It could not be determined if these had a red slip. From S2-L1 came a Papago bowl with a dark core and possibly a red slip.

	GLASS		Hardpaste White Earthenware							CERAMIC Porcelain		OTHER SPE		Bone	Knife Handle	Totals
	Stemware	Tumb.	Plate	Bowl	Bowl	Saucer	Cup	Pitcher	Unid. Form	Saucer	Cup	Mex.	Papago			
Trenches			1		2				1	1			2	2		9
S1-L1			2	3	1		1	1	2		1			6		17
S1-L2	2		3		1		2	1	4	1	1			12		27
S2-L1	3	1	3	1	1	1	1		1	5				6	1	24
S2-L2	1															1
Totals	6	1	6	4	4	3	3	3	2	8	2	1	8	26	1	78

Table 3.22

Feature 5 Food Preparation and Consumption Artifacts

Several of the hardpaste white earthenware forms have maker's marks. A plate with a cork stamped and handpainted floral, peasant ware decoration and a cup with a gold rim line, ca. 1876-present (Kovel and Kovel 1986: 257) came from S1-L1.

A T. and R. Boote marked dinner plate was found in S1-L2. This mark dates ca. 1890-1906 (Godden 1964: 84). In S2-L1 was a dinner plate with an Adam's mark, 1896-1914 (Godden 1964: 22); one plate has a C & A Meakin mark dating post-1890 that is not in Godden; and a saucer has a Thomas Hughes mark dating 1860-1894 (Godden 1964: 339). A plate with a cork stamped and hand painted floral decoration (peasant ware) also was found in S2-L1.

Architecture

Sixteen of the Feature 5 artifacts are architectural in function. These are a fired adobe brick fragment 1.5 in. thick, 3 5/8 in. wide, with the full length not present, recovered from the backhoe trench; window glass (2) and a ceramic doorknob from S1-L1; window glass (6) from S1-L2; window glass (3) and a fired adobe brick fragment from S2-L1; and window glass (2) from S2-L2. The adobe brick is roughly wedge shaped and is 1.81 in. thick, 3.88 wide, and 7.75 in. long. The two bricks found in Feature 5 are identical in color, shape, size, and method of manufacture to those from Feature 4 .

Leisure and Recreation

In the Leisure and Recreation category are 32 artifacts including soda, mineral water, beer, wine, and liquor bottles; a toy; two cartridges and a lead shot; and a phonograph record (Table 3.23).

In the backhoe trench material were three quart, hand finished beer bottles with base marks "I.G.Co", "C.V. CO. NO 2 MILW." and "M. G. Co." respectively. Two machine made 12 oz beer bottles, a machine made wine bottle embossed "ROMA WINES" with a Latchford-Marble base mark, and a soda bottle embossed "HERVE CARBON J.F.I. TUCSON" came from S1-L1. In S2-L1 was one beer bottle with an I.G. CO. base mark.

The I.G. CO. bottles date ca. 1870-1895 (Toulouse 1971: 261), the C. V. CO. dates 1880-1881 (Toulouse 1971: 151), the M. G. CO. dates either 1898-1911 or ca. 1895-1904 (Toulouse 1971: 359-360), and the Latchford-Marble dates 1939-1957 (Toulouse 1971: 332). The Hutchinson stopper dates 1879-1912 (Holsher 1965: 34-35) and may have come from the soda bottle.

		Backhoe	S1-L1	S1-L2	S2-L1	S2-L2	Total
Soda and Mineral Water	Soda Bottle	1	1	1			3
	Hutchinson Stopper		1				1
	Mineral Water Bottle	1			1		2
Alcoholic Beverages	Beer	3	2	3	6		14
	Wine	1	3	1	1		6
	Liquor				1		1
Toys	Doll Cup				1		1
Firearms	Cartridge		2				2
	Lead Shot		1				1
Other	Phono. Record		1				1
Total		6	9	7	10	0	32

Table 3.23

Feature 5 Leisure and Recreation Artifacts

The two cartridges are a .22 Short and a probable .38 caliber. The .22 dates from before the Civil War to the present and the .38 dates from ca. 1877 to the present (Barnes 1972: 163).

The toy is an undecorated porcelain doll cup from S2-L1.

Medical and Health

Only two artifacts related to this function were recovered, a prescription ware bottle from the backhoe trench and a proprietary product bottle from S1-L1. Neither had embossed lettering.

Personal

The personal artifacts are detailed in Table 3.24. For the most part these artifacts are female related. The bone tooth pick, the mirror, and the buttons could have been used by either sex. The shoe was too fragmented to determine the sex of the intended wearer.

Transportation

Only one artifact, a horseshoe, could be placed in this category. It was from S2-L1.

Tools and Hardware

The 73 artifacts in this category are listed in Table 3.25. All but three are nails.

Miscellaneous

In S1-L1 are a tin can and prehistoric flake; in S1-L2 are three tin cans, nine flakes and an unidentified seed; four tin cans, three flakes, and a bottle cork are from S2-L1; and in S2-L2 are a tin can and three flakes.

		Backhoe	S1-L1	S1-L2	S2-L1	S2-L2	Total
Personal Care	Florida Water Bottle					1	1
	Mirror		1	2		1	4
	Rouge Box	1					1
	Bone Toothpick				1		1
Clothing, Adornment	Clothing Button		2	2	4		8
	Bead		1				1
	Small Buckle		1				1
	Glass Pendant			1			1
	Shoe				1		1
Total		1	5	5	6	2	19

Table 3.24
Feature 5 Personal Artifacts

		Backhoe	S1-L1	S1-L2	S2-L1	S2-L2	Total
Nails	Unid.				9	4	13
	Square Cut	1	6	8	6		21
	Wire		12	24			36
Bolt					2		2
File				1			1
Totals		1	18	33	17	4	73

Table 3.25
Feature 5 Tools and Hardware

Unidentified

Forty artifacts could not be assigned to a specific function. The only datable item was a piece of turned pink glass, ca. 1919 to 1940s (see Feature 2 discussion) from S1-L2.

Summary Feature 5

The existence of several artifacts from the pit related to women, including the Florida water bottle and a glass necklace pendant, along with the child's toy porcelain cup, suggest that a family with a female child was responsible for the deposition of the Feature 5 trash that was in the pit.

That domestic activities occurred on this lot is supported by the presence of food related artifacts, including faunal remains (beef feet), and food preparation and consumption artifacts. In the latter category are one Mexican and five Papago bowls used for cooking purposes.

Three of the Papago bowls are clearly from the pit. These support a conclusion that the pit fill was deposited by a Mexican family living on Lot 7.

The Mexican bowl, two of the Papago bowls, the rouge box, a bead, a clothing slide, and some food and food preparation and consumption artifacts were from S1-L1 or were recovered from the back dirt during backhoe trenching. These artifacts could be either from the upper pit fill or from the sheet trash that covered the pit after it had been filled. If these are from the sheet trash layer, they would suggest a source similar to that of the pit fill.

Dating

Relatively few of the Feature 5 artifacts were datable (Fig. 3.12).

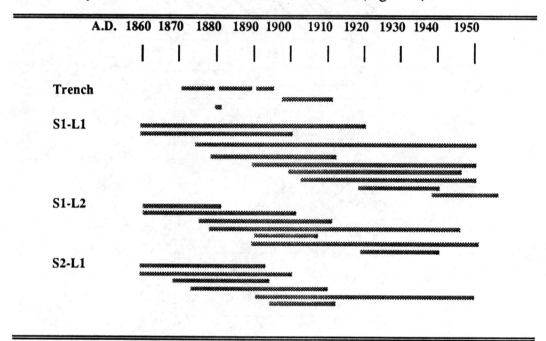

Figure 3.12
Feature 5 Artifact Date Ranges

All of those from S1-L1 can be accounted for within a range of 1912 to 1919 with the exception of a Latchford-Marble Glass Company bottle with a mark dating after 1939. The presence of this bottle along with a piece of plastic probably results from demolition and construction activities on this lot.

The level designated S1-L2 has artifacts that can be subsumed within a 1890 to 1900 date range. This accounts for all the artifacts except a piece of stemware with a pontil scar (ca. 1850 to 1880) and a piece of turned pink glass (ca. 1919 to the 1940s). The stemware object could easily have been an old piece that was broken during the suggested time range. The turned pink fragment clearly does not fit in this level; it is the only late artifact from S2-L2. It is probably an intrusive piece.

All the artifacts found in S2-L1 can be accounted for within a date range of 1894 to 1896.

The S1-L2, S2-L1, and by inference S2-L2, artifacts appear to date from the early mid-1890s to about 1900. Thus the pit may have been filled over approximately six years. The S1-L1 artifacts clearly suggest that much of, if not all of, S1-L1, is sheet trash that was deposited after the pit was filled.

Feature 6

This feature was discovered in the west wall of Trench 12 during the testing phase. It was located in Lot 7 at the rear of the house on South Main Street. It was not plotted on the Sanborn maps. After the removal by backhoe of the 12 in. thick layer of redeposited caliche and soil placed over the lot during construction of the Convention Center parking lot, a 6 ft. by 9 ft. rectangular area was excavated to expose the full horizontal extent of the feature. At 17.5 in. below the surface (bottom of S2-L2) the 6 ft. diameter feature was revealed in the top of the caliche (Fig. 3.13).

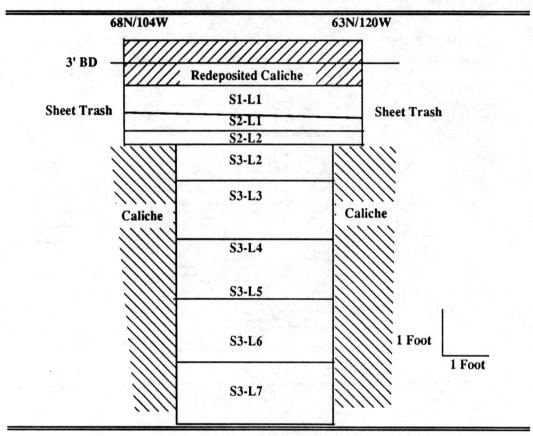

Figure 3.13
Feature 6 Profile

Initially, Feature 6 was thought to be another pit of the type represented by Feature 4, but its depth quickly revealed it to be a well. There was no evidence to suggest that this feature, like Feature 15, originally had been a pit like Feature 4 and then dug deeper to create a well. Feature 6 was a well from its beginning. The sides of the well were not strickly vertical but were alternately belled out and then contracted. No evidence of a structure around the top of the well was found.

Levels S1-L1, S2-L1, and S2-L2 were excavated over the entire 6 ft. by 9 ft. rectangle. When the top of the well was located at the base of S2-L2, excavation continued within the confines of the 6 ft. diameter well. The field notes suggest the possibility that the top of the well was actually at the top of level S2-L1 but because this layer appeared to be part of an extensive sheet trash deposit, it was not possible to separate the two.

The first level, S1-L1, was 7 in. to 9.5 in. deep and consisted of grey-brown sandy silt with some ash, charcoal, and artifacts. Included in the artifact assemblage were a few pieces of modern plastic (bags and the like), and several recent bottles which were not collected.

The next level, S2-L1, consisted of a reddish brown compact sandy silt with some ash and charcoal. The depth of this layer was from 3.5 in. to 6 in. Artifacts included modern plastic toy eye glasses, a piece each of green and yellow plastic, and a piece of cloth. S2-L2 was a mottled grey brown sandy silt with ash and charcoal that was 2.5 in. deep.

The levels within the confines of the well shaft, S3-L2 through S3-L7, were essentially similar. The fill was a brown sandy silt containing ash, charcoal. and artifacts. All six of these levels were more or less 2 ft. in thickness. There was no level designated S3-L1. The well was excavated to 14 ft. 4 in. below the surface after the removal of the parking lot paving, where excavation ceased for safety reasons. Probing revealed that the well continued at least another 2 ft. If the well actually began at the base of S1-L1, its overall depth would have been about 12 ft. 8 in. plus the depth below the base of S3-L7.

Artifacts

A total of 227 whole and fragmentary artifacts representing a minimum of 755 individual items was collected from nine levels (Table 3.26).

	Food	FP&C	H&F	Arch.	L&R	M&H	Pers.	Trans.	T&H	Misc.	Unid.	Totals
S1-L1												
Glass		1		1	3						5	10
Ceramic		4										4
Metal			1	1					4		2	8
Other												0
Total	0	5	1	2	3	0	0	0	4	0	7	22
S2-L1												
Glass	2	2		1	3						8	16
Ceramic		12			4							16
Metal		1		1	4				34		3	43
Other					1		1		1	6	4	13
Total	2	15	0	2	12	0	1	0	35	6	15	88
S2-L2												
Glass		1		1								2
Ceramic		6										6
Metal												0
Other										5		5
Total	0	7	0	1	0	0	0	0	0	5	0	13
S3-L2												
Glass	1	1		2	3	4	5				5	21
Ceramic		19	1		1							21
Metal					3		1	2	82	1	6	95
Other					1		4			18		23
Total	1	20	1	2	8	4	10	2	82	19	11	160
S3-L3												
Glass		1		1	2	4	3				4	15
Ceramic		12	1	2								15
Metal		1		1					50	1	3	56
Other												0
Total	0	14	1	4	2	4	3	0	50	1	7	86

Table 3.26
Feature 6 Artifacts by Function

(Continued next page)

(Continued from previous page)

	Food	FP&C	H&F	Arch.	L&R	M&H	Pers.	Trans.	T&H	Misc.	Unid.	Totals	
S3-L4													
Glass		2		2	1	1	2				3	11	
Ceramic		18	1		1							20	
Metal							3		59	1	3	66	
Other	1						5			29	3	38	
Total	1	20	1	2	2	1	10	0	59	30	9	135	
S3-L5													
Glass	3	4		2	3	4	3					6	25
Ceramic		28	1										29
Metal		3					2		28	1	3	37	
Other							1			24		1	26
Total	3	35	0	3	3	4	6	0	28	25		10	
	117												
S3-L6													
Glass	2	3	1	2	1	3						2	14
Ceramic		14	2										16
Metal								1	10	1	1	13	
Other							1			9	3	13	
Total	2	17	3	2	1	3	1	1	10	10		6	56
S3-L7													
Glass	4	1		1	3	2	3					7	21
Ceramic		15		2	1								18
Metal			1						33	1	2	37	
Other	1						1			19		21	
Total	5	16	1	3	4	2	4	0	33	20		9	97
TOTAL	14	149	8	21	35	18	35	3	301	116		74	774

Table 3.26
Feature 6 Artifacts by Function

Food

From S2-L1 is a food jar and an SCA catsup bottle, 1880 to 1919 (Ayres 1984: 128). In the fill of the well were found a food bottle (S3-L2); a corn cob (S3-L4); two condiment or spice bottles and a square food bottle (S3-L5); and a food bottle, probably part of one of the condiment bottles above, and an olive oil bottle (S3-L6). In S3-L7 are five food artifacts: a corn cob, a plain food bottle, one food bottle marked "CB", and two Wocestershire bottles marked "ACB Co." on their bases. The "CB" possibly represents Crosse and Blackwell an English food packager dating from 1830 (Toulouse 1971: 113). The Worcestershire bottles date 1849 to 1877 (Zumwalt 1980: 169). In the same category is an edible *Anadonta califoriensis,* probably from the Santa Cruz River.

Food Preparation and Consumption

In this category are 149 glass, ceramic, and metal artifacts from all levels of Feature 6 (Table 3.27).

Material	Form	S1-L1	S2-L1	S2-L2	S3-L2	S3-L3	S3-L4	S3-L5	S3-L6	S3-L7	Total
Glass	Water Bottle						1				1
	Stem Ware			1	1	1	1	3	1	1	9
	Tumbler		2								2
	Bowl							1	1		2
	Cup	1									1
	Mug							1	1		2
Ceramic: Hardpaste Wh. Earthenware	Dinner Plate				2		2	1	1	1	7
	Plate					1					1
	Bowl					2	2	2			6
	Serving B.		2					1			3
	Covered B.					1		1			2
	Saucer		3				1	1		1	6
	Cup				2		1	2		2	7
	Rect. Tray							1			1
	Unid.	1	2	1	4	1	3	3	1	3	19
Ceramic: Porcelain	Bowl		1		1	1					3
	Saucer								1	2	3
	Cup	1			1			1			3
	Unid.							1			1
Ceramic: Yellowware	Teapot					1					1
Ceramic: Softpaste Earthenware	Mexican				3	2	3	10	5		23
	Papago	2	4	5	6	3	6	3	6	6	41
Metal	Plate							1			1
	Bone Handle Knife					1					1
	Wood Handle Knife							2			2
	Mixing Spoon		1								1
Total		5	15	7	20	14	20	35	17	16	149

Table 3.27
Feature 6 Food Preparation and Consumption Artifacts

Four ceramic forms were marked. In S1-L1 is a C. C. Thompson and Company mark dated 1883-1890 (Gates and Ormerod 1982: 2882). From S2-L1 is a Furnival and Sons mark dated 1871 to 1890 (Godden 1964: 263). In S3-L2 are a Homer Laughlin Golden Gate pattern porcelain bowl with a gold rim line, ca. 1905 (Gates and Ormerod 1982: 133) and a hardpaste white earthenware dinner plate with a blue transfer printed floral design marked "JUNIATA PAT... UNDER... WARR... J. & E. (MAYER)". This probably dates from the 1890s to 1964 (Kovel and Kovel 1986: 234; Lehner 1980: 103). A cup of the same pattern is also from this level.

Other decorated ceramics include a porcelain cup with a blue rim line (S1-L1); an unidentifiable hardpaste white earthenware form with a brown printed floral design (S2-L1); a red printed design on the same type of form (S3-L2); a red painted design, also on an unidentifiable form, a peasant ware bowl, and a softpaste white earthenware teapot with a brown glaze (S3-L3); a peasant ware saucer and bowl (S3-L4); a peasant ware cup (S3-L5); and a peasant ware dinner plate, an unidentifiable flow blue form, and unidentifiable blue transfer printed form (S3-L7).

Finally in this category is a Papago cooking bowl with a dark core and a sooted exterior. It was probably once red slipped. A Papago plain brown, flat round tortilla warmer is also included. Both are from S3-L7 (see Table 3.21).

Household Furnishings

Eight artifacts were classified in this category. From S1-L1 was a metal drawer handle, possibly from a dresser or similar piece of furniture. In S3, levels 2, 3, 4, and 6 were pieces of an undecorated wash basin with a Baker and Company mark, 1839 to 1893 (Godden 1964: 51). These were counted as four separate forms but they probably represent only one basin. Additionally in S3-L6 are a softpaste white earthenware figurine of unidentifiable form and a milk glass vase with a glass tipped pontil scar. A kitchen range top cover with a lifter slot came from S3-L7.

Architecture

In the architectural category are 21 artifacts. Window glass panes were found in S1-L1, S2-L1, S2-l2, S3-L2(2), S3-L3, S3-L4(2), S3-L5(2), S3-L6(2), and S3-L7. A piece of covered electrical wire (S1-L1), a top of a drop cord bulb holder (S2-L1), and an electrical light bulb socket (S3-L3) represent artifacts associated with electricity. A ceramic door knob came from S3-L5. Small, red orange fired adobe bricks of the type identical to those from features 4, 5, and elsewhere were found in S3-L3 and S3-L7. The two in the former level are 1.75 in. by 3.63 in. by 7.25 in. and 7.50 in. in length. One in S3-L7 is 1.75 in. by 3.75 in. by 4+ in., and the other is 1.38 by 3.63 in. by 4+ in. in length. The fragments in S3-L7 were undoubtedly similar in length to those in S3-L3 and elsewhere from this site.

Leisure and Recreation

A total of 35 artifacts are classified in this category (Table 3.28). The wine and beer bottles from S1-L1 and the beer bottle from S2-L1 are of recent origin. The wine bottle was made by the Latchford Marble Glass Company and has "ROMA WINES" on its base, 1939-1957 (Toulouse 1971: 332). The beer bottle from S3-L5 has a crown finish and was machine made.

The fragments of dolls found in S2-L1, S3-L2, and S3-L4 are all porcelain. The specimen from S3-L2 has a green shirt or coat.

Cartridges were found in S2-L1 and S3-l2. Only those in S2-L1 had headstamps or were measurable. One, a shotgun shell, has "...W.R.A. Co." on it and three headstamps read "W.R.A. Co. .32-40". All four date approximately 1884 to 1940 (Barnes 1972: 47).

	ALCOHOLIC BEVERAGES					TOYS			FIREARMS	OTHER	Total
	Beer	Whiskey	Liquor	Wine	Wine/ Champagne	Doll	Porcelain Toy Cup	Toy Plastic Eyeglasses	Cartridge	Phono. Record	
S1-L1	1			2							3
S2-L1	2	1				2	2	1	4		12
S2-L2											0
S3-L2	2				1		1		3	1	8
S3-L3	1				1						2
S3-L4						1	1				2
S3-L5	1				1	1					3
S3-L6						1					1
S3-L7			1			2		1			4
TOTAL	7	1	1	5	5	4	3	1	7	1	35

Table 3.28

Feature 6 Leisure and Recreation Artifacts

Medical and Health

In this category are 18 bottles. Only one bottle, a proprietary, has legible embossed lettering. It has "HAMLINS WIZARD OIL" on its side. No meaningful dates were found for this product.

Personal

The 35 personal artifacts are listed in Table 3.29. Both men's and women's artifacts are present. The slate pencils are generally associated with children.

Transportation

Only three transportation related artifacts, a horseshoe and a horseshoe nail from S3-L2, and a horseshoe from S3-L6, were found in Feature 6.

Tools and Hardware

The 301 tools and hardware items are listed in Table 3.30. Nails account for 95 percent of the artifacts in this category.

Miscellaneous

There are 116 miscellaneous artifacts in Feature 6 (Table 3.31). The shells are a conus-type, and a possible Anodonta californiensis.

Function	Form	S1-L1	S2-L1	S2-L2	S3-L2	S3-L3	S3-L4	S3-L5	S3-L6	S3-L7	Total
Personal care	Cosmetic Bottle				1						1
	Mirror				1	1				1	3
	Brass Comb						1				1
	Bone Brush				1						1
	Tooth Brush									1	1
Clothing and Adornment	Button				5	2	5	2	1	2	17
	Suspender Fastener				1						1
	Garter Buckle							1			1
	Glass Bead						1				1
	Necklace Part				1						1
	Woman's Ring						1				1
	Woman's Brooch							1			1
Misc.	Bone Fan						1				1
	Slate Pencil				1		1	1			3
Total		0	1	0	10	3	10	6	1	4	35

Table 3.29
Feature 6 Personal Artifacts

Unidentified

Of the 755 artifacts from Feature 6, 74, or nearly 10 percent, were unidentifiable as to function. Included are three pieces of recent plastic material from S2-L1 and a piece of SCA glass from S3-L7 dated 1880 to 1919 (Ayres 1984: 128).

Summary Feature 6

The artifacts from the sheet trash levels above the well shaft in Feature 6 are obviously a combination of historic and relatively recent trash.

The recent trash is undoubtedly remains left from the demolition of the historic buildings on Lot 7 which disturbed the historic surface and subsurface in this area. Mixed with the historic artifacts are pieces of plastic and recent wine and beer bottles in S1-L1, and plastic toy eye glasses and fragments of plastic in S2-L1. No recent artifacts were identified in S2-L2.

	Unid .Nail	Sq. Nail	Wire Nail	Iron Wire	Copp Wire	Wood Screw	Bolt	Carr Bolt	Stove Bolt	Fen-ile	Iron Buc-kle	Iron Rod	Swi-vel Hook	Bat-tery Core	Total
S1-L1	3					1									4
S2-L1		5	27					1	1					1	35
S2-L2															0
S3-L2		32	46	1		1	1			1					82
S3-L3		28	21								1				50
S3-L4	56						2					1			59
S3-L5	28														28
S3-L6		9					1								10
S3-L7		31			1								1		33
Total	87	105	94	1	1	2	4	1	1	1	1	1	1	1	301

Table 3.30
Feature 6 Tools and Hardware

	S1-L1	S2-L1	S2-L2	S3-L2	S3-L3	S3-L4	S3-L5	S3-L6	S3-L7	Total
Tin Can				1	1	1	1	1		5
Shell						2				2
Seed				4			1			5
Charred Burlap								1		1
Rubberized Cloth				1						1
Obsidian						1				1
Carved Stone Decoration						1				1
Prehistoric Flake		6	5	12		24	23	8	19	97
Prehistoric Mano						1				1
Prehistoric Metate				1						1
Flashlight Bulb									1	1
Total	0	6	5	19	1	30	25	10	20	116

Table 3.31
Feature 6 Miscellaneous Artifacts

Given the disturbance in the main sheet trash levels, not much can be said about the trash in them. As is the case elsewhere on Lot 7, the presence of toys, women's and other artifacts suggests that this trash originated in a domestic habitation context.

The food, food preparation and consumption, household furnishings, and personal artifacts from the well fill generally reflect trash that would have originated from domestic household activities.

A number of artifacts relate to women and children. These include: a doll, a slate pencil, and part of a necklace from S3-L2; a doll, a slate pencil, a glass bead, a woman's ring and a bone ribbed fan from S3-L4; a slate pencil, a bottle once containing a cosmetic product, a garter buckle, and a woman's pin or brooch from S3-15; and a toy porcelain cup from S3-L7.

The women's and children's artifacts plus the Mexican and Papago ceramics, especially those used for cooking purposes, indicate that this trash originated from a Mexican family living on Lot 7. Mexican-made ceramics were found only within the well, shaft proper; Papago ceramics were found in all levels. Papago ceramics that were clearly used for cooking purposes were a bowl wih a sooted base and a tortilla "warmer." The latter is a circular, nearly flat, form used over a stove or open fire for cooking tortillas. Both of these artifacts came from S3-L7.

Dating

Most of the Feature 6 levels had too few datable artifacts to assign firm dates but some idea of possible dates can be provided (Fig. 3.14).

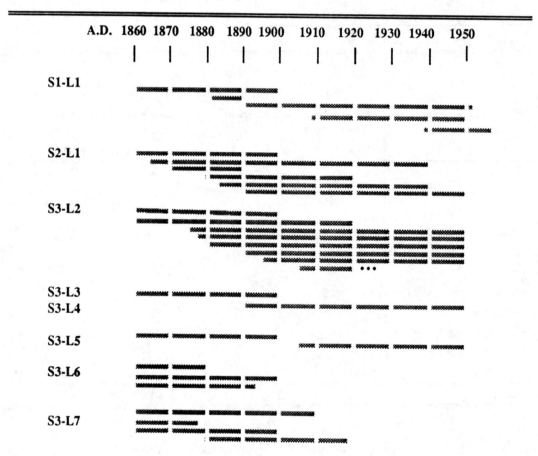

Figure 3.14
Feature 6 Artifact Date Ranges

For the sheet trash levels, S1-L1, and S2-L1, a date of 1900 to 1909 accounts for all the artifacts except two ceramic objects whose end dates are 1890. These artifacts were probably used until broken and discarded sometime after 1900. Mixed with the historic artifacts in these levels are a number of 1939 to ca. 1970 plastic, bottles, and similar material. No datable artifacts were found in S2-L2.

The fill in the well can be divided into two segments for dating purposes. The artifacts in the upper four levels, S3-L2 through S3-L5, date after 1903 based on the presence of a machine made beer bottle in S3-L5. All the artifacts in these levels can be accounted for within a range of 1903 to 1907. Thus they appear to be roughly contemporary with the historic artifacts in the sheet trash.

The bottom two levels, S3-L6 and S3-L7, appear to be substantially earlier than those above them. A date range of 1877 to 1880 accounts for all the dated artifacts.

If these dates reflect reality, then it appears that the well was filled through S3-L6 over 20 years before the S3-L5 trash was deposited after 1903. The filling of the well and the deposition of the sheet trash appears to have occured over a relatively short span of time or approximately between 1903 and 1909.

Feature 7

A privy pit labeled Feature 7 was found in Lot 7 in the northeast corner of what once had been the backyard of 313, later 315, South Main Street. This privy was shown on Sanborn's 1883 through 1896 maps of Tucson. It was not shown on the 1901 map (Fig. 3.8).

The pit was discovered in the west wall of Trench 12 during the testing phase. The trench cut across and removed the east end of the pit down to approximately the top of S3-L2.

The dimensions of the 3 ft. 2 in. deep pit were 4 ft. east-west and 7 ft. 3 in. north-south. Because of time constraints, the west 3 ft. of the pit were not excavated.

Overlying the pit was an approximately 7 in. layer of redeposited soil and caliche that was under the blacktop paving of the parking lot. This layer was removed with the backhoe. Under this material was a partially disturbed sheet trash level of dark brown sandy, highly organic soil, about 11.5 in. in depth. This was excavated as Stratum 1. This level, at least its upper part, was cut into during the demolition and construction activities on this lot. The artifacts reflect the mixing in that historic artifacts as well as more recent ones were found. The top of the feature begins at the base of this level.

Sometime after its abandonment, it appears that the fill in the pit subsided and subsequently the resultant depression was filled with trash including ash, charcoal, and artifacts. A depression would not be present in a typical privy pit while in use. This deposit was designated Stratum 2. It was excavated as a single 1 ft. 10 in. deep level within the confines of the pit. Stratum 2, which appeared to be undisturbed, contained 52 percent of the artifacts found in Feature 7.

S3-L1 and L2, both undisturbed levels, were around and below Stratum 2. S3-L1 was a silty, greenish brown, organically rich level containing ash, charcoal, and trash. It was a 2 ft. 1 in. deep level into which Stratum 2 extended 1 ft. 10 in.

The fill in S3-L2 was similar to that in S3-L1 except that the only artifacts it contained were three pieces of faunal material.

Artifacts

A total of 479 whole and fragmentary artifacts representing a minimum of 172 individual objects (Table 3.32) were recovered from the excavation of Feature 7. These are 28 from S1-L1, 89 from S2-L1, and 55 from S3-L1. No artifacts were recovered from S3-L2. In addition, 334 whole and fragmentary faunal remains were recovered (Table 3.33). All the bones from this feature were analyzed.

	Food	FP&C	HF	Arch.	L&R	M&H	Pers.	T&H	Misc.	Unid.	Totals
S1-L1											
Glass			3		4		1				8
Ceramic		5									5
Metal								12		1	13
Other									2	1	3
Total	0	5	3	0	4	0	1	12	2	2	29
S2-L1											
Glass	2	3	1	2	7	10	4			2	31
Ceramic		13		1	3					3	20
Metal	1	2	1		6			19	3	2	25
Other				1			8		4		13
Total	3	18	2	4	16	10	12	10	7	7	89
S3-L1											
Glass	1		2	2		7				7	19
Ceramic		9			1					7	19
Metal		1		1				8	1	2	18
Other							3		10		13
Total	1	10	3	2	1	7	3	8	11	9	55
TOTALS	4	33	8	6	21	17	16	30	20	18	173

Table 3.32

Feature 7 Artifacts by Function

Food

Only four food artifacts were found in Feature 7. These are a general food jar, a can key, and a barrel mustard jar from S2-L1. Part of the mustard jar was found in S3-L1. The two tin cans listed below as Miscellaneous artifacts may have been food containers.

In addition to the artifacts noted above, 334 pieces of fauna were collected. Only 72 of these are clearly food related. They represent the remains of two doves, a chicken, a goat, and three beeves.

Of the 72 pieces of bone, 46 (64 percent) are beef. The cuts of meat indicated by these pieces include short loin and round (S1-L1), short loin and shoulder (S2-L1), and shoulder and fore shank (S3-L1).

Bones from beef feet, which were used for making menudo, were found in S1-L1 (1) and S2-L1 (29). None were found in the privy pit fill. In general the beef bones from Feature 7 represent the cheaper cuts of meat.

Undoubtedly many of the 208 bones listed in Table 3.33 as small to large mammals and in the unidentified category are from beef and other edible animals. At least 18 bones in the mammal category and two in the unidentified category show evidence of having been butchered.

Species	Indiv.	S1-L1	S2-L1	S3-L1	S3-L2	Total
Food Species						
Columbia cf livia (Rock Dove)	2		1	22		23
Gallus gallus (Chicken)	1		1	1		2
cf Capra hircus (Goat)	1				1	1
Bos taurus (Beef)	3	6	34	6		46
Total	6	36	29	7	1	72
Other						
Knosternon sp. (mud turtle)	1			5		5
Aves (bird; eggshell)	1		1			1
Sciuridae (unidentified squirrel, etc.)	1		3	1		4
Sigmodon sp. (Cotton Rat)	1		4			4
Neotoma sp. (Wood Rat)	3		5	5		10
Felis domesticus (Domestic Cat)	1		25	4		29
Homo spaiens (human)	1	1				1*
Small to Large Unidentified Mammals		10	17	41	2	70
Unidentified		7	93	38		138
Total		18	148	94	2	262

*pre or neonatal ulna fragment

Table 3.33

Feature 7 Faunal Remains

Food Preparation and Consumption

The 33 artifacts in this functional category are listed on Table 3.34. A plate from S1-L1 has a partial Homer Laughlin mark and is decorated with rose decals, 1896 - ca. 1930 (Gates and Ormerod 1982: 128). From S2-L1 is a porcelain saucer with a hand painted overglaze floral decoration and a pink rim line, and a brown floral transfer decorated dinner plate with an incomplete registry mark dating 1868-1883 (Godden 1964: 527). Also from S2-L1 is a saucer with a Maddock and Co. mark dating 1906 - present (Godden 1964: 405, No. 2466). S3-L1 contained a small plate with an impressed James Edwards and Sons mark dating ca. 1851-1882 (Godden 1964: 231).

	GLASS		CERAMIC						Porcelain	SPE	METAL		
			Hardpaste		White Earthenware								
	Stemware	Tumbler	Dinner Plate	Small Plate	Soup Plate	Saucer	Cup	Unid. Form	Saucer	Papago	Fork	Tblsp.	Total
S1-L1			1		1	1	1			1			5
S2-L1	3	1	6			1	1	1	1	2		2	18
S3-L1			1	1			1			6	1		10
TOTALS	3	1	8	1	1	2	3	1	1	9	1	2	33

Table 3.34

Feature 7 Food Preparation and Consumption Artifacts

Household Furnishings

Eight artifacts were placed in this category. In S1-L1 is a mirror, an SCA pressed glass object, and a clear cut glass object with a ruby overlay. The decoration is cut through the overlay. Both of these objects are vases or similar forms. The SCA piece dates 1880 to 1919 (Ayres 1984: 128). S2-L1 contained a kerosene lamp chimney and a furniture key, and S3-L1 two kerosene lamp chimneys and an alarm clock.

Architecture

Artifacts with an architectural function are two window panes, an electrical fuse, and a fragment of plaster or lime from S2-L1 and two window panes from S3-L1.

Leisure and Recreation

In this category are 21 artifacts. In S1-L1 are four wine bottles. Three of the S1-L1 bottles are embossed "ROMA WINE" and have the Latchford-Marble maker's mark dating 1939 to 1957 (Toulouse 1971: 332). S2-L1 contains a toy marble, a toy cup, one wine bottle, five beer bottles, two ceramic bottles once containing ale or a similar product; and six cartridges. A third ceramic bottle came from S3-L1. Two of the beer bottles from S2-L1 have maker's marks. One has a C. C. Conrad monogram, ca. 1876 to 1883 (Toulouse 1971: 117) and one has L G Co on its base, ca. 1880 to 1910 (Toulouse 1971: 323). The cartridges were a probable .32 caliber and five probable .41 caliber cases without headstamps. The .41 caliber cases date 1877 to 1930 (Barnes 1972: 165). The .32 caliber dates about 1878 to the present (Barnes 1972: 154).

Medical and Health

Medical and Health related artifacts consist of prescription ware and proprietary medicine bottles. In S2-L1 are eight prescription ware and two proprietary bottles. Two of the prescription bottles have base marks, a "W" in a diamond and McC Co. The former is undated but the latter dates 1841 - ca. 1886 (Toulouse 1971: 351). One of the proprietary bottles is embossed "DR. J.G.B. SIEGERT & HIJOS".

S3-L1 contains six proprietary bottles and a prescription ware bottle. Three of the proprietary containers are embossed, "DAMIANA BITTERS BAJA CALIFORNIA", which are undated, and one proprietary has "P.D.& Co." on its base, 1875-present (Toulouse 1971: 417).

Personal

Artifacts in this category total 16. In S1-L1 is a shoe polish bottle with "WHITTEMORE BOSTON U.S.A." embossed on it. Four glass buttons, a rubber douche set, a hard rubber syringe (possibly from the set), three shell buttons, a bone comb, a bone button, and a slate pencil are from S2-L1. The syringe has "GOODYEAR" impressed into its side. Personal artifacts from S3-L1 are a hard rubber syringe, part of a rubber douche set, and a hard rubber comb. The Goodyear product dates from 1852 when Goodyear patented his vulcanizing process.

Tools and Hardware

The 30 artifacts in this category are all nails. Three square cut and nine wire from S1-L1, two square and eight wire from S2-L1, and four square, one wire, and one unidentified from S3-L1.

Miscellaneous

The artifacts in this category (Table 3.35) are two tin cans, a bucket ear, a type font, a piece of coal, and 15 prehistoric flakes.

Unidentified

Eighteen artifacts were unidentifiable. Included in this category are a piece of plastic, a piece of SCA glass, 1880 to 1919 (Ayres 1984: 128), and a bottle with an Owens Illinois Pacific Coast Co. marker's mark and the year code "48" which indicates the manufacture date as 1948 (Toulouse 1971: 406). All of these artifacts are from S1-L1.

	Tin Can	Bucket Ear	Type Font	Coal	Prehistoric Flake	Total
S1-L1				1	1	2
S2-L1	1	1	1		4	7
S3-L1	1				10	11
TOTAL	2	1	1	1	15	20

Table 3.35
Feature 7 Miscellaneous Artifacts

Summary Feature 7

Feature 7 is a relatively shallow privy pit associated with the house on the west side of Lot 7. It appears to have had three depositional episodes, one of sheet trash that postdates the use of the privy (S1) one (S2) that represents fill within the slumpage depression created when the fill in the privy subsided, and the privy fill itself (S3).

Artifacts related to women and children are found only in S2 and S3. In S2-L1 was a marble, a toy porcelain cup, a hard rubber syringe and other parts of a douche or enema set. S3-L1 contained parts of a similar set. These were used primarily for the purposes of a woman's personal hygiene, but could also be used for giving an enema.

These artifacts suggest that both the S2 and S3 deposits in Feature 7 were a result of family activity. There is no way to determine if the deposits resulted from one, or more than one family.

The food, food preparation and consumption, household furnishings, and the leisure and recreation and personal artifacts support the suggestion that a family, possibly with both a male and a female child, was responsible for the deposition of the trash in S2. There is no evidence that children were present in the family responsible for the trash in S3.

There is very little evidence from which to determine the ethnic background of the users of this feature. There were no Mexican-made ceramics in Feature 7 and very few Papago vessels represented.

The Papago forms consisted of three ollas, one in each level, and two smaller jars one each in S2 and S3-L1. All were red slipped with a dark carbon core. No cooking bowls were found.

The absence of Mexican-made ceramics and Papago bowls used for cooking purposes suggests the possibility that at least some of these deposits, notably the actual latrine fill (S3), might be of Anglo origin. All but one of the beef feet bones used for making menudo were found in S2. One came from S1. Because menudo is primarily a Mexican dish, it is likely that the S2 deposit is of Mexican origin.

Dating

There were not enough datable artifacts from S1 and S3 to provide strong support for the interpretation that they were three episodes of deposition involving Feature 7 (Fig. 3.15).

This privy is shown on the Sanborn fire insurance maps from 1883 through 1896 which suggests that it was used during this period.

All that can be said for S1-L1 is that the historic trash in it appears to date sometime ca. 1900. In this level were found two machine made bottles dating respectively 1939 to 1957 and 1948. These clearly were deposited as a result of demolition and construction activities on the block. No other machine-made bottles were found in Feature 7.

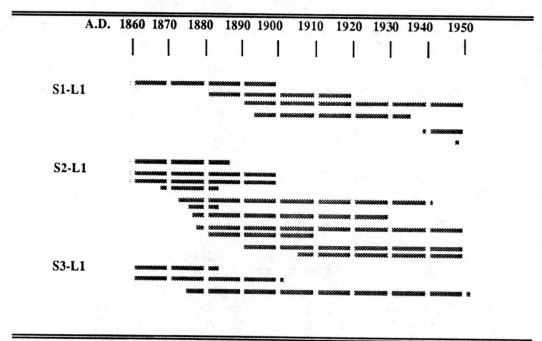

Figure 3.15
Feature 7 Artifact Date Ranges

With one exception, the S2-L1 artifacts can all be accounted for within the years 1883 to 1890, and conceivably they could date within an even more restricted range of 1886 to 1890. The one exception, a Maddock and Company saucer dating 1906 to the present, is probably an intrusive artifact that belongs with the S1-L1 artifacts. There is no possibility that S2-L1 could date as late as 1906.

In Stratum 3 only Level 1 contained datable artifacts. This, like S1-L1, had so few datable artifacts that only a general date of ca. 1883 could be derived for it.

The datable artifacts suggest that though it is shown on the 1896 Sanborn map, the privy was not in use at that time.

Feature 11

Feature 11 was a relatively shallow, natural depression below a large area of relatively thin sheet trash that appears to cover much of the center of Block 228. Overall, the depression measured about 4 ft. east-west and 10 ft. north-south. It lay on the south side of Feature 4 and west of Feature 15 in the center of Lot 7 at the rear of the house designated 313, and later 315, South Main Street. The depression was discovered in backhoe Trench 6 during testing.

A 5 ft. by 6 ft. rectangle was excavated on the eastside of Trench 6 in two levels, one, S1-L1, was the overlying sheet trash and the other, S2-L1, was the depression below it. Overlying these levels was a 12 in. thick layer of sterile caliche and soil placed there during construction of the Convention Center. This material was removed by backhoe before excavation began.

The level excavated in the sheet trash and designated S1-L1 was about 9 in. in depth and that labeled S2-L1 was about 10.5 in. thick. S1-L1 covered the entire 5 ft. by 6 ft. excavation, but S2-L1 had an irregular east edge that was encountered from about 1 ft. to 2.5 ft. east of Trench 6. Both levels consisted of silty soil mixed with ash, charcoal, and artifacts.

The depression (S2-L1) had an irregular bottom with a nearly 2 in. thick layer of fine silt and clay in its lowest parts.

In the east central part of S1-L1 at 12 in. to 14 in. below the surface was a pit and a posthole. These were designated features 12 and 13 respectively. No artifacts were found in either of these two features. Both appear to be intrusive into S1-L1.

Feature 12 was about 5.5 in. deep, about 14 in. in diameter, and was 14 in. below the surface. The pit contained a very organic fine silt. Its purpose could not be determined.

The posthole, Feature 13, was found 12 in. below the surface at the top of S1-L1. Its diameter was 6 in. and its depth 1 ft. 7 in. Decomposed wood was found in it. The purpose of this post is unknown.

Upon completion of the excavation of Feature 11, the west edge of Feature 15 was noticed at the east edge of the 5 ft. by 6 ft. excavated rectangle. About 2 ft. of the diameter of Feature 15 showed in Feature 11.

Artifacts

Feature 11 produced a total of 357 whole and fragmentary artifacts representing a minimum of 107 individual items (Table 2.36). S1-L1 contained 54 and S2-L1 53 of these.

Food

Only two food artifacts, two condiment or pickle bottles, both from S2-L1, were found in Feature 11. The tin cans listed under the Miscellaneous category may also have been food containers.

Food Preparation and Consumption

Artifacts related to this function totaled 32. From S1-L1 are one stemware glass, one piece of porcelain of unidentifiable form, pieces of hardpaste white earthenware representing two unidentifiable forms, two Mexican-made unidentifiable forms, and four Papago pieces, including two bowls, a jar, and one unidentifiable form.

S2-L1 contained an unidentifiable form of hardpaste white earthenware, nine Mexican forms, and 13 Papago forms. The Mexican vessels are five bowls, one jar, two unknown, and a handle. Papago forms are nine bowls and four jars. One of the Papago bowls from S2-L1 was used for cooking purposes.

	Food	FP&C	HF	Arch.	L&R	M&H	Pers	Trans	T&H	Comm	Misc	Unid	Total
S1- L1													
Glass		1	1	1	2	1	5					2	13
Ceramic		9		1								1	11
Metal					4		1	1		9	1	5	21
Other			1	1							9		11
TOTAL	0	10	2	3	6	1	6	1	0	9	10	8	56
S2- L2													
Glass	2				2		2					2	8
Ceramic		23	1										24
Metal									9	1	1	1	12
Other							1				8		9
TOTAL	2	23	1	0	2	0	3	0	9	1	9	3	53
TOTAL	2	33	3	3	8	1	9	1	9	10	19	11	109

Table 3.36

Feature 11 Artifacts by Function

Household Furnishings

In this category are a kerosene lamp chimney and a possible fragment of linoleum from S1-L1. S2-L1 produced a plain hardpaste white earthenware chamber pot lid.

Architecture

The three architecture related artifacts from Feature 11, a piece of plaster, a piece of a window pane, and half a red orange fired adobe brick, were found in S1-L1. The brick is 1.75 in. thick and 4 in. wide. One face is slightly concave. This brick is identical in form, color, and size to those from features 4 and 5.

Leisure and Recreation

S1-L1 has one wine bottle, one beer bottle dating ca. 1880 to 1910, and four center fire cartridges without headstamps. One of these is a .45-70, two are .41 caliber, and one is a .450 revolver cartridge. These date 1873 to 1930, 1877 to 1930, and 1868-1940 respectively (Barnes 1972: 63, 165, 173).

A wine bottle and a toy marble with two cutoff scars are from S2-L1. The marble dates 1880 to ca. 1905 (Randall 1971: 104-105).

Medical and Health

Only one artifact, an unmarked proprietary medicine bottle from S1-L1, could be placed in this category.

Personal

Personal artifacts from S1-L1 are four milk glass buttons, a wound green glass bead, and a metal button. From S2-L1 are a milk glass button; an opaque, purple, wound glass bead; and a slate pencil.

Tools and Hardware

The only artifacts in this category are nine square cut nails found in S2-L1.

Transportation

A horseshoe nail from S1-L1 is the only transportation related artifact.

Communication

In this category are nine pieces of metal type from S1-L1 and one from S2-L1.

Miscellaneous

From S1-L1 are a tin can, a lead foil bottle top seal, seven prehistoric flakes, and a prehistoric mano.

S2-L1 contained a tin can and eight prehistoric flakes.

Unidentified

Eleven artifacts, eight from S1-L1 and three from S2-L1, could not be assigned to a specific function.

Summary Feature 11

Feature 11 is a relatively shallow depression used for trash disposal purposes and is associated with the house on the west side of Lot 7. The feature probably represents two depositional episodes, one in the depression (S2-L1) and one, a sheet trash deposit (S1-L1), of a longer duration overlying it. The source of the artifacts in S2-L1 may have been different than for those in S1-L1, but because no firm dates could be established for the two strata, this remains uncertain.

Only a few artifacts, the beads in both levels and the slate pencil and marble in S2-L1, suggest the presence of women and children on the property. These artifacts, plus the food preparation and consumption and household furnishings objects, indicate a domestic family origin for these deposits.

The presence of both Mexican and Papago ceramics, including a Papago bowl from S2-L1 used for cooking purposes, suggests that the family or families, depositing the Feature 11 trash were of Mexican ethnic background.

Dating

So few datable artifacts were found in Feature 11 that assigning firm dates to the two strata is not possible. Based on the artifacts that are dated, a date range of about 1880 to 1910 applies to S1-L1. The lone S2-L1 date is about 1880 to 1905.

Feature 15

This feature, similar in form to those labeled features 4, 5, and 17, was found in Lot 7 in what had once been the backyard of 313, later 315, South Main Street (see Fig. 3.8). The circular, or rather D-shaped, vertical sided pit, which was dug into solid caliche, was located by Trench 12 during backhoe testing.

Feature 15 began as an 8 ft. diameter pit that was about 6 ft. deep. At the bottom of the pit, at 10 ft. 8 in. below datum, a roughly 6 ft. by 8 ft. rectangular pit, had been excavated through the floor. Thus, it appeared that the feature was originally a circular pit that later was excavated deeper to create a feature with a new function, possibly that of a well.

Situated over the pit was a relatively sterile, 11 in. thick level of sheet trash labeled S1-L1 that was removed by shovel and not screened. It contained reddish brown sandy silt with some small gravel and a few very small fragments of artifacts. None of these was collected. Over this level was a sterile layer of redeposited caliche and soil about 1 ft. in depth. This layer was removed with the backhoe and was under the parking lot paving.

The pit fill was a relatively homogeneous brown sandy silt that contained virtually no stove ashes and only a few artifacts. Holes or small "tunnels" in the wall similar to those in features 4, 5, and 17 were noted. Four were about 6 in. in diameter and one had a maximum diameter of 10 in. Three of the small holes were generally angled to the north, one was 6 ft. 8 in. below datum in S2-L1, one was at 8 ft. 9 in. in S2-L2, and one was at 9 ft. 7 in. in S2-L3; the shallowest was angled toward Feature 4. One small hole was located on the west side 10 ft. 6 in. below datum in S2-L3. The 10 in. hole was 8 ft. 2 in. below datum in S2-L2 and angled to the southeast. At 10 ft. 8 in. below datum the rectangular pit was discovered; only a remnant of the floor of the circular pit remained.

S2-L4 was removed by backhoe. The walls of the upper pit showed several examples of pick marks made during its original excavation.

Artifacts

The excavation of Feature 15 produced a total of 461 whole and fragmentary artifacts representing a minimum of 172 individual objects (Table 3.37).

	Food	FP&C	HF	Arch.	L&R	M&H	Pers.	Trans.	T&H	Comm.	Misc.	Unid.	Total
S2- L1													
Glass	1	1	1		2	1	2					1	9
Ceramic		7									1		8
Metal		1			1				12			2	16
Other							1				14		15
Total	1	9	1	0	3	1	3	0	12	0	15	3	48

Table 3.37
Feature 15 Artifacts by Function

(Continued next page)

														Total
S2- L2														
Glass		1		1	3	3					1		3	12
Ceramic		15										1		16
Metal								1	6		1			8
Other												10		10
Total	0	16	0	1	3	3	0	1	6	1	12		3	46
S2- L3														
Glass		1		2	5								3	11
Ceramic		7			1									8
Metal								3	8		1		3	15
Other												17		17
Total	0	8	0	2	6	0	0	3	8	0	18		6	51
S2- L4														
Glass	1	2		1	9	2								15
Ceramic		8												8
Metal								2				1	1	4
Other														0
Total	1	10	0	1	9	2	0	2	0	0	1		1	27
TOTALS	2	43	1	4	21	6	3	6	26	1	46		13	172

Table 3.37

Feature 15 Artifacts by Function

(Continued from previous page)

Food

Only two food bottles were found in Feature 15, a Worcestershire sauce bottle in S2-L1 and a pickle or condiment bottle in S2-L4. The sauce bottle dates 1877 to 1920 (Zumwalt 1980: 269). The tin cans listed under the miscellaneous category may also have been food containers.

Food Preparation and Consumption

The 43 artifacts in this category are detailed in Table 3.38. Included in the glass is an SCA stemware form, 1880 to 1919 (Ayres 1984: 128) from S2-L1 and two turned pink stemware forms dating ca. 1919 to 1940s (see Giarde 1980: 164) from S2-L2 and S2-L3.

A porcelain plate from S2-L1 has a gold rim line, 1876 to present (Kovel and Kovel 1986: 257) and a turquoise overglaze decoration.

S2-L2 produced an unidentifiable hardpaste white earthenware form with a blue transfer printed decoration.

An unidentifiable porcelain form from S2-L4 has a gold rim line dating as that in S2-L1. An unidentifiable hardpaste white earthenware form (S2-L4) has a brown transfer printed decoration and a small plate has blue transfer printed floral clusters. This plate has "JUNIATA

PATTERN UNDER GLAZE WARRENTED J.& E. MAYER" on its base. The Mayer firm was in business from 1881 to 1964 (Lehner 1980: 103).

The Mexican and Papago forms are thought to have been used for purposes of food preparation and consumption. A sooted Papago cooking bowl came from S2-L4.

Material		Form	S2-L1	S2-L2	S2-L3	S2-L4	Total
Glass		Stemware	1	1	1	2	5
Ceramic	Hardpaste White Earthenware	Soup Plate		1			1
		Small Plate				1	1
		Bowl		1			1
		Cup	2	1		2	5
		Unidentified Form	1	4	1	2	8
	Porcelain	Small Form	1			1	2
		Saucer Plate			1		1
		Unidentified				1	1
	Softpaste Earthenware	Mexican Form		1			1
		Papago Form	3	7	5	1	16
Metal		Dinner Fork	1				1
Totals			9	16	8	10	43

Table 3.38

Feature 15 Food Preparation and Consumption Artifacts

Household Furnishings

A kerosene lamp chimney from S2-L1 is the only artifact in this category.

Architecture

A piece of a window pane from S2-L2, two panes from S2-L3, and one pane from S2-L4 constitute the artifacts in the architectural category from Feature 15.

Leisure and Recreation

Mineral water bottles were recovered S2-L1 (1), S2-L3 (1), and S2-L4 (1). These probably represent only one bottle. One soda bottle with a Hutchinson stopper, 1879 to 1912 (Holscher 1965: 34-35) was from S2-L3. Wine bottles were found in S2-L1 (1), S2-L2 (2), S2-L3 (2), and S2-L4 (2). A lead foil seal from a champagne bottle is labelled "G.H. MUMM & CO ..." It came from S2-L1. Beer bottles were located in S2-L1 (1), S2-L2 (1), S2-L3 (1), and S2-L4 (6). Two of those from S2-L4 are labelled "S.B. & G. CO." and date 1881 to 1905 (Toulouse 1971: 461) and two have "A.B.G.C. ST.L." on their bases. This mark is not listed by Toulouse but it may be one of Adolphus Busch's marks when he operated a glass factory in St. Louis from 1904 to 1928 (Toulouse 1971: 26).

A solid porcelain doll originally 3 in. to 3.5 in. in height came from S2-L3.

Medical and Health

Unmarked proprietary bottles were found in S2-L1 (1), S2-L2 (3), and S2-L4 (1). A turned pink prescription ware bottle came from S2-L4. This dates ca. 1919 to the 1940s (see Giarde 1980: 164).

Personal

Personal artifacts are a hand mirror, a school slate board, and a woman's glass button, all from S2-L1. The button is opaque purple, 25 lignes in size, and has a molded design of a rose bush hanging over a picket fence. Originally the exterior was gold covered.

Transportation

A horse harness snap hook (S2-L2), a copper harness rivet burr, and a muleshoe (S2-L3), and two horseshoes (S2-L4) make up the transportation artifacts.

Tools and Hardware

Square cut nails dating about 1860 to 1900 came from S2-L1 (12), S2-L2 ·6), and S2-L3 (7). A piece of iron pipe also came from S2-L3.

Communication

An ink bottle labeled "CARTER'S" came from S2-L2.

Miscellaneous

The 46 artifacts in this category are detailed in Table 3.39.

	Tin Can	Shell	Tumacacori Poly	Prehist. Sherd	Flake	Prehist. Sherd	Prehist. Mano	Pinto Point	Totals
S2-L1		1	1	11			1	1	15
S2-L2	1			10	1				12
S2-L3	1			16			1		18
S2-L4	1								1
TOTAL	3	1	1	37	1		2	1	46

Table 3.39
Feature 15 Miscellaneous Artifacts

The shell in S2-L1 is an unidentified type probably from the Gulf of California.

Surprisingly, a piece of Spanish or Mexican period Tumacacori polychrome was found in S2-L1.

Bruce Huckell identified forty-one of the artifacts as prehistoric, including sherds, flakes, a mano, and a Pinto point dating ca. 4000 to 5200 B.P.

Unidentified

Thirteen artifacts could not be assigned a function. These include a piece of turned pink glass from S2-L3 dating ca. 1919 to 1940s (see Giarde 1980: 164).

Summary Feature 15

The configuration of this pit is different from the other pits on this lot in that, in its final form at least, it is D-shaped. It appears as though the original 6 ft. deep pit was circular in plan as were features 4, 5, and 17. Later a rectangular pit was excavated through the floor of the original pit. If that were the case, the easternmost two-thirds of the circular pit would have to have been squared up at the same time to create its D-shape plan. Squaring up the pit would seem to be a lot of extra and unnecessary work. It may be that the circular pit had been filled in prior to the excavation of the rectangular one, thus the second pit would ahve been excavated from the surface rather than from the floor of the circular pit.

The likely sequence of events for the creation of this feature was first the excavation of a circular pit, abandonment and filling of that pit, and finally the excavation of the rectangular pit from the surface through the circular pit. Holes, or small "tunnels" similar to those seen in the walls of the other circular pit features also were found in Feature 15. These occurred in both the wall remnant of the circular pit as well as in those of the rectangular pit above the original pit floor. The latter are undoubtedly remnants of holes that originally began at the wall of the circular pit.

The holes are found in solid caliche and are not the former locations of tree roots or rodent burrows. It is unclear whether ot not these are man-made.

Why there are so many holes in the walls of Feature 15 and what their purpose was is unclear. Originally it was thought that they connected one pit with another but a careful search of the area around Feature 15 failed to reveal other pits except Feature 17. None of the holes in Feature 15 head in the direction of that feature.

The artifacts found in Feature 15 were deposited when the rectangular pit was filled in apparently more or less at one time. Given the quantity of artifacts found, the feature appears not to have been used systematically as a trash dump. Fragments of one large green glass water bottle found scattered in three levels (S2-L1, S2-L3, and S2-L4) support the suggestion that filling occurred over a relatively short time period.

Generally speaking, the artifacts found in Feature 15 were similar to those found elsewhere in Lot 7. Both Mexican and Papago-made ceramics were found, including one Papago bowl used for cooking purposes. These suggest that individuals of Mexican descent were responsible for the trash (tables 3.20 and 3.21).

A school slate board, a porcelain doll, and a woman's fancy coat button indicate the presence of a family with at least one child. Whether one or more families were responsible for these artifacts is uncertain as is the origin of the trash. Presumably it came from the occupants of the west part of Lot 7 , but if the pit were filled with soil from off-site, the artifacts may have originated elsewhere.

Dating

The majority of the artifacts from Feature 15 appear to date about 1905 to 1910 (Fig. 3.16). The turned pink glass found in all Stratum 2 levels below S2-L1 dates later (ca. 1919 to the 1940s) than the 1905 to 1910 range (see Feature 2 discussion).

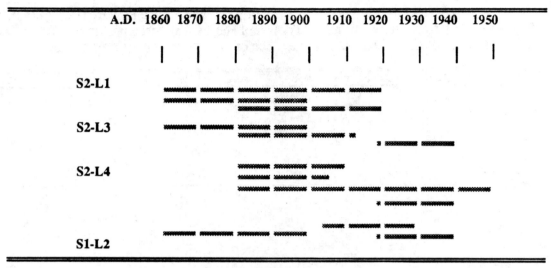

Figure 3.16
Feature 15 Artifact Date Ranges

The presence of the turned pink glass, which was probably surface debris because exposure to sunlight is necessary for it to turn color, suggests that the filling of Feature 15 occurred sometime ca. 1920 and that the other trash in the feature also may have been miscellaneous surface trash collected and deposited in the pit.

Feature 17

Feature 17 was located when it was decided to remove the layer of redeposited caliche and soil overlying the area south of Feature 15 to see if additional circular pits of the type seen at features 4, 5, and 15 could be located. This feature was the only one found as a result of that exercise (Fig. 3.8).

The feature was a circular, vertically sided pit, 5 ft. 1 in. in diameter, cut into solid caliche. Its depth was 28 in. to 36 in. with the north side being shallower. The top of Feature 17 was about 2 ft. 11 in. below the surface after the parking lot paving was removed. The feature was the southern most and shallowest of the four circular pits found in Lot 7. Like the others, it had small holes in its side walls suggesting a drain or similar function. In the northeast side the hole was about 4 in. in diameter and 6 in. below the top of the feature and on the southwest side is was about 4 in. in diameter and 23 in. below the top of the feature.

The fill of Feature 17 was a brown, loosely compacted sandy silt with some organic material and very few artifacts. It was removed in two levels, S1-L1 was 2 ft. in depth and S1-L2 was 11.5 in. on the south side and 4 in. on the north. The homogeneity of the fill and the paucity of artifacts suggests that Feature 17 was filled rapidly, and that it was not intended to be used for trash dumping purposes.

Artifacts

Only 32 artifacts representing a minimum number of 26 individual objects were found in Feature 17 (Table 3.40). S1-L1 had 16 and S1-L2 had 10 artifacts. The faunal material from this feature was not analyzed.

S1-L1 produced a piece of plain hardpaste white earthenware (Food Preparation and Consumption), a piece of a window pane (Architecture), a beer bottle (Leisure and Recreation), eight square cut nails (Tools and Hardware), four lithic flakes and a prehistoric plain ware sherd (Miscellaneous).

From S1-L2 came a piece of plain hardpaste white earthenware (Food Preparation and Consumption), four square cut nails (Tools and Hardware), three prehistoric lithic flakes and a prehistoric sherd (Miscellaneous), and a piece of dark green glass (Unidentified).

	FP&C	Architecture	L&R	T&H	Misc.	Unidentified	Total
S1-L1							
Glass		1	1				2
Ceramic	1				1		2
Metal				8			8
Other					4		4
Total	1	1	1	8	5	0	16
S1-L2							
Glass						1	1
Ceramic	1				1		2
Metal				4			4
Other					3		3
Total	1	0	0	4	4	1	10
TOTALS	2	1	1	12	9	1	26

Table 3.40
Feature 17 Artifacts by Function

Summary Feature 17

Too few artifacts were found in Feature 17 to determine what their origin might have been.

None of the artifacts are specifically datable. The beer bottle is of a type popular between about 1880 and 1910, and the square cut nails were used between 1860 and about 1900. Based on this slim information, a date of ca. 1900 should apply to the trash features.

Chapter 4

DATA INTEGRATION AND INTERPRETATION

Project Overview

The project's field work began in mid-March and was terminated in mid-May 1988. It was performed in two stages, a testing and subsequently a data recovery phase. This archaeological effort was confined to the area of a parking lot south of the present Convention Center Arena in former Block 228 and to a small area west of it in former Block 221. All of the significant historic remains were confined to lots, 6, 7, and 17 on Block 228. Lots 6 and 17 are considered together because they were bought and sold together from 1896 onward. Prior to 1896, Lot 17 was an unnumbered part of Lot 1.

A total of 17 features, 14 discovered during the testing phase and three located during data recovery, were evaluated for possible study. Features 1-11 and 14-16 were located during backhoe testing, and features 12, 13, and 17 were found during the subsequent mitigation efforts. Features 12 and 13 were found during excavation of Feature 11, and Feature 17 was located near the end of the project field work during a search for additional circular pits. Features 12 and 13 were inconsequential features containing no artifacts. Fourteen of the 17 features were excavated, features 3, 14, and 16 were not.

Lots 6 and 17 contained features 1, 2, 8, 9, and 10 and features 1-7, 11-13, 15, and 17 were within the boundaries of Lot 7. Each grouping of features was treated as being related to the lot on which it was found. This was only logical because none of the features predated the initial, formal occupation of the lots. This grouping facilitated the analysis of the artifacts by attempting to associate them with the various lot occupants over time. Table 4.1 provides a summary of the features, their lot numbers, dates, and possible family associations.

Most of the features studied were of the ordinary and expected variety. Features such as privies, wells, and trash pits of various dimensions and configurations were all anticipated and realized. What were not expected were the four circular pits, features 4, 5, 15, and 17, all in Lot 7. Pits of this type have not been reported or found previously. They are nearly circular in plan and generally have nearly vertical side walls and flat bottoms. All were dug into solid caliche hardpan. They ranged in size from 8 ft. in diameter and 6 ft. in depth (Feature 15) to 5 ft. in diameter and 3 ft. in depth (Feature 17).

The purpose or function of these pits could not be established although several suggestions relating to their probable use were advanced, including use as septic tanks and cisterns. Initially the holes in the pit sides were thought to be possible connecting "tunnels" between pits, but there were many more tunnels leading in a number of directions where there were no pits with which to connect. What or who created the tunnels is unknown. None of the pits produced evidence of a superstructure or other surficial structural elements.

It is unlikely that the pits were septic tanks. There was no sewer tile leading into them, and although demolition and preparation of the site for the parking lot disturbed the historic surface, it did not appear to have impacted the pits themselves. A similar, circular pit was found by Statistical Research, Inc. during excavations of a block some distance north of our project area, but sewer tile led into it. In that example, the sewer line was about 2 ft. below the present surface. Further, there was none of the noticeable staining that would be expected in a septic tank. The fact that Feature 15 was originally a circular pit that was later excavated deeper to create a well suggests that it did not serve as a septic tank. Even in an age where sanitation and the proximity of wells and latrines were not of great concern, it is unlikely that a well would have been dug through an existing or abandoned septic tank.

Feature Number	Type of Feature	Lot Association	Estimated Date of Filing	Possible Family Association	Remarks
1	Trash Pit	17	ca. 1929-1930	Unknown	
2	Large Trash Deposit	6 & 17	ca. 1890-1910	Brady	
3	Sheet Trash	7			Not Excavated
4	Circular Pit	7	ca. 1900	Von Erxleben	
5	Circular Pit	7	Mid 1890s-1900	Von Erxleben	
6	Well	7	1877-1890;1903-1907	Pre Von Erxleben	
7	Privy	7	1883-1890	Post Von Erxleben	
8	Pit	17	1919-1921	Pre Von Erxleben	
9	Pit	6	1900-1903	Unknown	
10	Privy	6	1894-1900	Brady	
11	Pit	7	1880-1900	Unknown	
12	Small Pit	7			No Artifacts
13	Posthole	7			No Artifacts
14	Small Pit	7			Not Excavated
15	Circular Pit	7	1905-1910	Post Von Erxleben	
16	Small Pit	7			Not Excavated
17	Circular Pit	7	Mid 1890s-1900	Von Erxleben	

Table 4.1

Dates and Family Associations of Residencesin Block 228

The pits, excavated into solid caliche, would have been nearly impermeable. Their use as water storage cisterns is a possibility. The holes in the pit side walls however seem to obviate their use as water storage tanks. The fact that a well was already present (Feature 6) on the lot also puts to question this suggested use.

It also has been suggested that the pits may have been tree wells. Given the proximity of the caliche hardpan to the surface, the trees would have had limited viability without room for root development. The so-called "tunnels" may have been made by roots but this is doubtful. There was no trace of wood either in the pits or the tunnels. Finally, the nature of the fill and the artifacts suggest that the pits were filled over a period of time with domestic trash rather than being filled during tree planting with some trashy fill. There appeared to be no backfilled caliche in these pits, a material one would expect given the circumstances.

It is possible that whatever their intended use, the pits were never actually used except for refuse disposal. At any rate, we may never know what use the pits had or were intended to have. No information as to who constructed these pits was located. Features 4, 5, and 17 all date from the mid-1890s to ca. 1900. Feature 15 dates about 1905 to 1910. The trash in the first three features dates to the period when Charles Von Erxleben lived on the property (1894 to 1904). As a civil engineer he may have been instrumental in the construction of the pits for some special purpose, but they easily could have been excavated years before the mid-1890s. The well created from Feature 15 may have been excavated by Von Erxleben or his predecessor but it was clearly filled after the former had moved from the property.

On lots 6 and 17, trash in three features (2, 9, and 10) appears to have been deposited by the Brady family (Table 4.1), although part of Feature 2 may predate the Brady occupation of the lot. Features 1 and 8 could not be assigned to a particular occupant of the property.

Artifacts found in three features (4, 5, and 17) seem to be associated with the tenure of the Von Erxleben family on Lot 7 (Table 4.1). The artifacts in the lower levels of Feature 6 appear to predate the Von Erxlebens and the upper levels may postdate their residency. Feature 7 predates the Von Erxleben occupation of Lot 7. The dating of the trash in Feature 11 is so general that associating it with a particular family is not possible, but some, if not all, may be from the Von Erxlebens. Finally, the artifacts in Feature 15 seem to postdate the Von Erxleben residency on Lot 7.

The 14 excavated features in lots 6, 17, and 7 produced a total of 11,396 whole and fragmentary artifacts. These represent a minimum of 3615 items. The artifacts and thus the excavated features appear to date within a relatively narrow timeframe. Table 4.1 presents the dates assigned each feature. Overall the trash yielded dates ranging from about 1877 to 1930. The earliest deposit, the lower levels of Feature 6, dated 1877 to 1880, and the latest deposit (Feature 1) dated to about 1929 to 1930. Most of the features date somewhere between 1890 and 1910. Feature 7 dates about 1883 to 1890. Feature 7 and the lower levels of Feature 6 are the only features on Lot 7 dating prior to 1890. These features, a privy and a well, were in use from the initial occupation of the lot. No deposits were found on Lot 6 that dated earlier than about 1890.

Historical and Architectural Overview

During the period 1880 to 1910 when most of the trash found on Block 228 was being deposited, Tucson was a small town, more Sonoran in appearance than most contemporary Arizona towns. In 1880, at the beginning of this period, the Southern Pacific Railroad arrived. This single event had a profound effect on the subsequent direction of Tucson's development. It spurred business creation and brought an influx of people from the east. In 1880 the population of Tucson was about 7000, a decade earlier it was less than half that at about 3200. The number of 1870 residents was about 3.5 times larger than the population in 1860. The 1880 figure was inflated because it included impermanent railroad construction crews. In fact the permanent population was much smaller than 7000.

By 1900 Tucson was "a small but important commercial center ... dominated by Anglo businessmen and Anglo politicians" (Sheridan 1986: 121). In fact less than a decade after the Gadsden Purchase, Anglo capital was well established (Sheridan 1986: 37). Most of the Mexican population of Tucson lived in barrios located south of the central business district, and most were employed as laborers and in other blue collar jobs. The residents of the barrios found that the Mexican owned stores scattered throughout these neighborhoods provided them with nearly everything they needed (Sheridan 1986: 99, 122). The residents of Block 228 appear to have enjoyed a similar situation with the variety of stores accessible to them along both sides of Meyer Street.

Sheridan (1986: 122) points out that there were two important considerations in the lives of most Tucsonans; where they lived and what jobs they held. With the gradual influx of Anglos, the population became one characterized by increasing stratification, both in terms of economics and of ethnicity. It was during the decade of 1900 to 1910 that the

Mexican population lost its majority status in Tucson (Sheridan 1986: 121). In 1900 the total population of Tucson was about 7500 and by 1910 it had grown to about 13,200.

Block 228 was developed after 1872 and with surrounding blocks experienced the changes described above. Although technically not falling within the boundaries of a formally named barrio, the block, at least its eastern half, probably functioned as though it was part of a barrio.

The first evidence of someone residing on Block 228 was in 1881, although the lots were first sold in 1872. Undoubtedly occupation began before 1881, at least on some lots. The Tucson city directory for 1881 indicates that both lots 6 and 7 were occupied (Barter 1881). The available historical documentation does not inform us as to who was living on these lots before 1881 or after 1883 to about the early 1890s. The lots were continuously occupied until late 1968 when all the buildings were demolished to prepare for the construction of the Tucson Convention Center.

Block 228 can be characterized as having both residential and commercial functions, but it was primarily a residential block. Table 2.2 details the business history of the block derived from the Sanborn maps.

For most of its existence, the population of Block 228 was probably predominately Mexican, at least on the east side. For Tucson as a whole, Mexicans made up about 71 percent of the population in 1860 but by 1920 this figure had declined to about 37 percent (Sheridan 1986: 3).

Interestingly, the east and west sides of the block exhibited many contrasting characteristics in architecture, in the use of space, housing types, density of occupation, and so on. The houses on the east side of the block were usually different than those on the west side. In general they were sited on the edge of the street, had only a small rear yard, and were most often found in rows of attached buildings, as in the Sonoran style. All the east side dwellings were constructed of adobe; brick was only used for a few commercial buildings. The streetscape would have appeared compact and mostly homogeneous to the viewer. The presence, and use of outdoor ovens on the east side as late as 1914 speaks to the differences between the two sides. No ovens were ever built on the west side. All the businesses were on the east side of the block, on Meyer Street, until relatively late in its life cycle. No businesses were located on Main Street except in about 1930 when a store was located on the southwest corner.

The west side can generally be characterized as one in which the houses were frequently constructed of brick, were not built to the street edge and had front and backyard space, were larger than those the east side, were fewer in number with only one to a lot, and had no businesses for neighbors. To the passerby, the west side would have presented a less unified and less harmonious streetscape than the east side. Ironically, the two exceptions to the east side pattern were the house on the east end of Lot 7 (324 South Meyer Street) and the one on Lot 6 (304 South Meyer Street). Both were detached houses and in both cases the property exhibited characteristics of both sides of the block. Overall the eastside of Block 228 was Sonoran in character and the westside appeared as a higher economic status area more characteristic of the Anglo parts of Tucson. In its later years both sides were predominately Mexican occupied.

Research Goals

The research goals of the Tucson Convention Center Expansion Archaeological Project included three general and ten more specific topics that were to be addressed using a combination of historical documentary sources and the artifacts recovered from the feature excavations (Ayres 1988c).

The three general goals, to establish the location of all the features within their appropriate historic lot boundaries, to prepare as detailed a history of each lot as possible, and to date the artifacts and subsequently the features from which they were obtained. These three tasks were completed and the information from them was used to assess the artifacts and features in terms of the more specific research topics and to integrate the archaeological with the historical data.

It was intended that project research would focus on food, dietary and consumer behavior, and food preparation activities represented by assemblages of artifacts from Block 228. These topics were expressed in more specific terms in the form of 10 questions for which the data including historical documentary information and the artifacts, and the faunal remains were expected to provide answers.

The reduction in the budget for artifact analysis precluded the possibility for a complete faunal analysis, which reduced the ability to make comparisons between most features and between the two lots.

Only the faunal remains from Feature 7 (a privy) and one level of Feature 5 (a circular pit) in Lot 7 could be studied, and Feature 10 (a privy) was the only deposit analyzed from Lot 6. These three proveniences accounted for 1072 pieces of fauna, 265 from Feature 5, 334 from Feature 7, and 473 from Feature 10. The dates for these features and their family associations are listed in Table 4.1.

100 percent of the other artifacts were identified and analyzed. These artifacts include glass, ceramic, metal, and others made of miscellaneous materials.

The 10 questions guiding this project's research are:

1. What was the variety of food types present and how did they vary through time?

2. Large quantities of butchered bone were recovered, does the butchering reflect Mexican or Anglo techniques, or both?

3. Do the food related artifacts and the faunal remains indicate that the inhabitants of these lots enjoyed a balanced diet?

4. Did wild game supplement the diet?

5. Was there a reliance on national and international sources for food rather than on local sources?

6. Is there evidence for increased reliance on eastern manufactured goods over those produced locally or regionally?

7. Specifically, what were the sources of food products for Tucson?

8. What was the role of the Papago and Mexican made ceramics in the households being studied?

9. Was the use of Papago and Mexican made ceramics confined to Mexican households?

10. Do the artifacts reflect a change in the use of the various lots over time?

For the purposes of analysis and discussion, the 10 questions can be grouped into a smaller number of related categories. Questions 1 and 5-7 relate to food types and sources, questions 2-4 to the fauna, and questions 8 and 9 pertain to Mexican and Papago ceramics. Question 10 is necessarily dealt with separately.

Underlying these questions was a basic assumption that both Anglo and Mexican generated trash would be found in Block 228 and that it would reflect cultural differences between the two groups, especially in the area of the food behavior.

Questions 1 and 5-7: Food Variety and Food Sources

In its early history, local agriculture played a prominent role in providing food for the residents of Tucson. The Santa Cruz River floodplain west of Tucson was farmed extensively, generally through the use of small scale irrigation systems. At the time of the Gadsden Purchase and later, Tucson was an agrarian community relying heavily on the results of farming to feed itself. Livestock, including beef, sheep, goats, and fowl, was also an important source of food. Hunting and collecting of wild plant resources were undoubtedly a part of everyday life.

During the two decades flanking the turn-of-the-century, agriculture was still of importance in meeting the local demand for food. The arrival of the railroad in 1880 probably hastened the change from one of dependence on a locally produced and acquired food supply to one of increasing reliance upon outside sources for commercially prepared foods. The growing influx of outsiders to Tucson during this period over burdened the local agricultural system; procuring food supplies grown or manufactured elsewhere became a necessity.

Reliance on home grown foods, on livestock raising, on hunting, on collecting from the Santa Cruz River (shell collecting and fishing), and on collecting wild plant resources declined over the years but most, except food from the river, never really died out. Generally, collecting depended on the family's economic status, and to some extent, on family tradition. Collecting was decidedly more important to the Mexican families than to the Anglo families. In the Santa Rita Mountains, for example, acorns, walnuts, wild grapes, mesquite beans, "little limes", various cacti, and many other plants were exploited for a variety of foods (Ayres 1984: 534), wild honey also was gathered. Collecting of plant foods continues to the present.

A wide variety of trees were planted to produce quince, pomegranate, fig, peach, and other fruits. Other locally produced food included barley, wheat, corn, beans, and a wide range of vegetables. Hunting, to supplement the diet, would have produced deer, rabbit, antelope, a variety of birds, and javelina, and more. From the river area came fish, water fowl, and the edible bivalve Anodonta californiensis.

Most of the food resources described above would leave little that would remain in an archaeological context except the faunal remains and some fruit seeds. Commonly used, and locally produced, flour, beans, other vegetables, and most wild plant foods would not leave remains.

Within the artifact assemblages from lots 6, 17, and 7 were a number of food related items, mostly faunal remains. Most features contained few food related artifacts of the canned or bottled variety. Fresh meat, mainly beef, was obviously an important food source to the residents of these lots.

Food related artifacts found in the features were: fruit jars; food bottles and jars whose specific contents are unknown; milk bottles from levels near the surface; condiment, sauce, and pickle bottles; cans known to have contained food; shell; two corn cobs; extract bottles; and a peach seed. Probably many of the tin cans whose contents are unknown, and which were classified in the Miscellaneous artifact category, were food cans. All in all a rather limited variety of food related artifacts were recovered. Not counting fauna and unknown tin cans, only 102 food related artifacts were found in the 14 features.

The most numerous of these artifacts were food bottles and jars whose contents were unknown. Of these, 91 percent were from Feature 10. Condiment, sauce, and pickle bottles made up the next most numerous category. At least one of these bottles came from all the features except features 1, 4, 8, and 17. In fact, no food related artifacts were found in features 4 and 17.

As suggested above, the early sources of food consumed in Tucson were essentially local. After the arrival of Anglos, and especially after the appearance of the railroad, the reliance on local sources of food gradually decreased while the reliance on food shipped into the city from elsewhere in the United States, and even from international sources increased.

Except for the minor features, most features were filled between about 1890 and 1910. During this 20 year period there is no evidence that Tucson businesses manufactured packaged foods. All the food artifacts that had identifiable embossed labels originated (with one exception) in the midwest or east. As far as can be determined, the only marked containers that were filled in Tucson were soda, milk, and pharmacy bottles.

Among the food bottles and jars, only 12 were labeled with an identifiable product or packager mark. All contained condiments, such as catsup, mustard, and Worcestershire sauce, or extracts for food flavoring. Four of these were packaged in New York, four in Chicago, one each in Philadelphia, Cincinnati, and San Francisco, and one, and possibly two, were packaged in England.

The relative paucity of store purchased food items suggests that more food of the types that do not survive in archaeological contexts might have been used. Although a wide variety of packaged foods were available in Tucson when the trash in the lot 6, 17 and 7 features was deposited, personal preferences, costs of commercially packaged foods, and the availability of locally produced food products may explain the limited quantity of these artifacts.

Questions 2-4: Fauna

Beef, sheep, goat, pig, and chicken were the preferred animals eaten for food. Of these, beef represented 94 percent of the remains of edible fauna in Feature 5, 64 percent in Feature 7, and 52 percent in Feature 10. Sheep and goat represented only 4 percent in Feature 5, 1 percent in Feature 7, and 15 percent in Feature 10. Pig and chicken were only infrequently represented.

Henry (1987: 370-371) has discussed the beef fauna recovered from excavations in Phoenix, Arizona, in terms of the relative cost of various butchering units. Enough beef remains were found in the Tucson excavations to classify some of them in similar terms (Table 4.2). The ranking of cuts is based on Henry (1987: 370), as are the approximate turn-of-the-century prices assigned to them.

Beef Cut	Feature #5	Feature #7	Feature #10	Average Price/Lb.
Hindshank	8		1	$ .59
Feet	5	3	3	.69
Neck	2		3	.88
Frontshank	2	2	4	1.57
Chuck	4		7	1.81
Rump	15		11	2.32
Round	5		6	2.67
Ribs	2	2	5	3.33
Loin	12	3	5	3.69

Table 4.2
Beef Butchering Units Ranked By Cost

Table 4.2 data do not indicate clear cut differences between features 5 and 10 beef remains. Not enough units were present in Feature 7 to make meaningful comparisons. Both features 5 and 10 contained more cuts costing over two dollars per pound than under two dollars per pound. Feature 7 had only one cut, beef feet, that cost less than one dollar per pound. None of the beef feet bones from Feature 7 showed signs of butchering while those in the other two features did. The feet in Feature 7 were probably discards rather than food remains.

Feature 5 trash was generated by an Anglo family, while Feature 10 represents mixed Anglo and Mexican trash. It is thought that Feature 7 trash also originated from an Anglo family. Interestingly, on the basis of the beef, not much difference is exhibited between features 5 and 10. Also of interest is the fact that butchered foot bones, traditionally used by Mexicans to make menudo, were found in both features 5 and 10.

In addition, wild game was present in all three of the features. Deer was found in Feature 5, dove in Feature 7, and fish and duck in Feature 10. Other wild game traditionally utilized for food in Tucson included antelope, javelina, rabbit, and quail. Oyster shells were present in features 2 and 8 and an example of Anodonta californiensis, an edible fresh water mollusc, came from Feature 6. A peach seed was found in Feature 10. These plus the packaged food and the fauna mentioned above suggest that the residents of lots 6, 17, and 7 enjoyed a reasonably good and varied diet. Nothing in the artifacts from any of the 14 features excavated suggested anything out of the ordinary in terms of food. All indicate that the residents of these lots were consuming much the same food items as their neighbors elsewhere in Tucson at the time.

Questions 8 and 9: Mexican and Papago Ceramics

Mexican and Papago ceramic forms were widely used in Tucson for utilitarian purposes, such as storage, cooling of drinking water, cooking, and the serving of food, before about 1920. Papago pottery is still available today but it generally is used for nonutilitarian, decorative purposes. Even today, Mexican made ceramics are used in many households, although none of the types found archaeologically are still used. Large Papago jars, or ollas, were very common and were used by Anglos and Mexican alike for cooling drinking water through evaporation. Beyond the use of ollas, little is known of the use of other Papago ceramic forms by Anglos; they may have been used for a number of purposes, however.

A basic assumption about Mexican and Papago ceramics was that Mexican households in Tucson were more likely to use a combination of Mexican and Papago forms than were Anglos. The tentative conclusions provided with the artifact descriptions were written with this in mind. The economic status of the household might have an effect as to who actually used these ceramics. For example, less affluent Anglos might have emulated the Mexican use patterns. Mexican use of Papago ceramics extended to several cooking forms, especially use of bean pots, as well as water ollas, and food serving, and food storage pieces. Anglo use of Papago ceramics was thought to have been more restricted and was primarily confined to ollas that facilitated the cooling of drinking water.

Ceramic forms, mostly bowls, thought to have been used for cooking purposes were identified as such by the presence of exterior sooting. Sooted vessels were usually of Papago manufacture but some Mexican made forms were also sooted.

The Mexican made ceramics were bowls and some jars; the majority were a pale green glazed, relatively highly fired redware. Some vessels had small handles or lugs and some rims had finger made depressed grooves like those on a homemade pie crust. Many of the Mexican ceramics forms were decorated with a metallic dark brown floral decoration that was applied by hand. Exactly where in Mexico these ceramics were produced is not known.

The Papago ceramics were commonly bowl and jar forms, often with a red slip and horse manure temper that created a dark carbon streak within the body of the vessel. Many bowl forms were of plainware without the dark core or a slip. Very few of the red slipped forms were decorated and all the Papago pottery tended to be rather friable. Most of the Papago vessels were likely made at San Xavier.

Papago pottery was found in all 14 features with the exception of Feature 17. Mexican redware was not found in features 1, 7, or 17. Fragments of at least 10 Mexican made forms were found in features 2, 6, 10, and 11. The same quantity of Papago forms were found in features 2, 4, 5, 6, 9, 10, 11, and 15 (Table 3.5 and 3.21).

Mexican bowls with sooted exteriors were found only in features 2, 5, and 10 (Tables 3.4 and 3.20). Papago bowls used for cooking were not found in Feature 1, the upper levels of Feature 6, or in features 7 and 17. In the lower levels of Feature 6 were both a Papago cooking bowl and a round, nearly flat tortilla warmer. Tortilla warmers are approximately 14 in. to 18 in. in diameter and are known from other urban Tucson archaeological sites.

In the Lot 6 proveniences (features 2, 9, and 10) dating to the Brady occupation, a minimum of 94 Mexican and 104 Papago vessels were found. Feature 4, 5, 11, and 17 dating to the Von Erxleben tenure on Lot 7 produced 22 Mexican and 63 Papago forms.

The post-Brady trash from features 1 and 8 contained two Mexican and eight Papago forms. Pre Von Erxleben features (Feature 7 and the lower levels of Feature 6) contained five Mexican and 21 Papago forms, and the post Von Erxleben proveniences (Feature 15 and the upper levels of Feature 6) had 19 Mexican and 45 Papago forms.

The ratio of all Mexican to Papago forms in the features dating to the Brady occupation of Lot 6 is 1 to 1.1, and of the cooking vessels 1 to 2.1. In the proveniences dating to the Von Erxleben presence on Lot 7 the ratio of all Mexican to Papago forms is 1 to 2.9 and for cooking bowls 1 to 10. These figures indicate that the Bradys used about an equal number of Mexican and Papago ceramic forms in their household, and that for every one Mexican cooking bowl used, two of Papago manufacture were used. For the Von Erxleben family the relationship between the two ceramic types is not so close. This family preferred Papago ceramics in general nearly 3 to 1 and for cooking purposes they used 10 Papago vessels for every Mexican bowl used.

Preference for Papago forms over Mexican forms appears obvious in both the Brady and the Von Erxleben cases. In the other proveniences predating and postdating these families, the same relationship is found. Why this was the case is not clear, but the Papago forms were undoubtedly more readily available, and were probably cheaper than those of Mexican manufacture. Also the Papago forms were much more friable and thus more easily broken and so had to be replaced more often.

The apparent differences in preference between Mexican and Papago ceramics by the two families may be cultural, economic, or may simply be a result of the vagaries of trash deposition and archaeological recovery.

Brady was a miner by occupation according to the 1900 federal census, Von Erxleben was a civil and mining engineer who at one time served as a U. S. mineral surveyor. On the basis of occupation Von Erxleben must have ranked higher but Brady must have held relatively high status in the community because he was a well known and respected Arizona pioneer. There is nothing, either in the historical record or in the archaeological data, to suggest that one or the other was the more affluent or was held in higher esteem in the community.

The intensity of testing and data recovery was similar for the two lots. The trash deposits provide a good quantity and variety of artifacts from both families although no Von Erxleben latrine was found. They may very possibly have had indoor plumbing when they lived on Lot 7.

If we assume that the differences in terms of Mexican and Papago pottery was not a result of trash deposition and recovery factors, and that the two families enjoyed essentially the same status, why the differences? One assumption of this project was that Mexican families were more likely to have both Mexican and Papago pottery available for everyday household use than would Anglo families. The Brady household included a number of Mexican women who undoubtedly were responsible for all the food preparation in the household. The Von Erxleben family included no Mexicans. It seems reasonable to conclude that the differences can be accounted for by the presence of Mexican women on Lot 6. At the same time, it would appear that the Von Erxleben family was using and cooking with both Mexican and Papago ceramic forms, but to a lesser extent than the Bradys. It is clear that the use of Mexican and Papago ceramics for cooking and other uses was not exclusive to Mexican families during the 1890 to 1910 period in Tucson.

Question 10: Change in Lot Use

The historical records and the archaeological data do not provide much assistance in understanding the change in lot use over time. Historical records were, however, more useful than were the archaeological remains. Clearly the lots were always predominately residential in use as was the block on which they were located. Only one business, the 1883 Heredia fruit store, was located on Lot 6. Apparently the store operated for a very short time, possibly for less than one year. No feature was located on Lot 6 that dated to the Heredia occupation in 1883. No business was located on Lot 7, but the house on South Main Street was formally made into an apartment building sometime between 1914 and 1919 and served as such for many years. All in all, the two lots were remarkably stable in use and in their architectural styles throughout their existence.

Other Considerations

In addition to the research questions discussed above, a look at the presence of artifacts related to women and children may also be useful, as would a review of some of the hardpaste white earthenware forms, to help establish economic rankings of lot occupants. In addition, a brief mention of the prehistoric artifacts is made below.

Women's and Children's Artifacts

Women's artifacts included buttons, clothing parts, jewelry, cosmetics, and items of personal care. Doll dishes, slate boards and slate pencils, marbles, dolls, a harmonica, and a toy animal eye were the children's artifacts.

Both women's and children's artifacts were found in features 2, 5-7, 10, 11, and 15. Only children's artifacts were found in Feature 9, and features 1, 4, 8, and 17 contained none of these artifacts.

Women's and children's artifacts were found in those features (5 and 11) dating to the Von Erxleben family's occupation of Lot 7. None of these artifacts were found in Von Erxleben features 4 and 17. This family had a boy and a girl; their presence is reflected in the toys and school slate boards and pencils found in features 5 and 11.

The Brady features (2, 9, and 10) on Lot 6 also produced women's and children's artifacts. All three features produced children's objects, and all but Feature 9 contained women's artifacts. There were four children in the Brady household, a girl and three boys, and more than one adult female. The toys present in the trash appearing to date to the Brady's occupation are very similar to those from the Von Erxleben features. The girl's toys were a doll and numerous toy dishes; the boy's toys were marbles and a harmonica. A school slate board and a slate pencil also were found in the Brady trash.

Features 6, 7, and 15 also contained women's and children's artifacts. The trash in features which predated and postdated the Von Erxleben presence on Lot 6 apparently also originated from families.

Ceramic Ranking

Henry (1987: 369) provides turn-of-the-century cost figures for ceramics in Phoenix. She indicates that undecorated hardpaste white earthenwares were the least expensive and that porcelain forms were the most expensive. The forms with molded decoration and with transfer printed or decal decorations fall in between, as shown on Table 4.3. The differences in ceramic costs between Phoenix and Tucson would be negligible. Henry lumped the transfer printed and the decal decorated types together. Their relative costs were essentially identical. These two types may have been used and broken together but they were not necessarily made or purchased at the same time. Decal decorated ceramics became popular after the decline in interest in the transfer printed forms.

The cost estimates are used to evaluate four categories of plain and decorated hardpaste white earthenwares and porcelain represented by four common forms, cups and saucers as sets, bowls, and plates. The cup and saucer sets were more expensive than were the bowls, and the plates were the least expensive. The porcelain category includes both decorated and undecorated examples. It was thought that evaluating these ceramics with known costs, might provide additional insight into the lifestyles of the Brady and Von Erxleben families. Only Brady features 2, 9, and 10 and Von Erxleben features 4, 5, 11, and 17 are considered.

Table 4.3 clearly indicates a preference in both families for the plain undecorated hardpaste white earthenwares. In terms of the printed and decal decorated hardpaste white earthenware forms, only the Brady family apparently had them to discard. None were found in the Von Erxleben proveniences. The Brady family also discarded more porcelain forms and had a wider range of decorated and porcelain forms than did their neighbors.

	Cup & Saucer Sets	Bowls	Plates
Undecorated (HWE)			
Brady	11	13	30
Von Erxleben	3	9	9
Molded Decoration (HWE)			
Brady	1	3	1
Von Erxleben			
Transfer or Decal Decorated (HWE)			
Brady	3	8	2
Von Erxleben			
Porcelain			
Brady	2	3	
Von Erxleben	2		

Table 4.3
Ceramics in the Brady and Von Erxleben Households

One explanation for the differences is that the Brady's lived on Lot 6 for a longer time and had a larger family than did the Von Erxlebens on Lot 7. The Brady's lived on the block for about 14 years with a household of about eight individuals, the Von Erxlebens lived on Lot 7 for 10 years with a household size of about six people including two boarders. Nonetheless, the differences appear to be so great that the short time involved and the differences in household size would seem to be a minor factor. One decorated form not considered by Henry was the cork or sponge stamped, handpainted peasant ware. Two plates of this pottery were found in Von Erxleben Feature 5. While no definite conclusions can be made from Table 4.3, tentatively it would seem that the Brady family might have been more affluent than the Von Erxleben family.

Prehistoric Artifacts

Prehistoric artifacts were found during the course of excavation of every feature except in minor features 1, 12, and 13. These artifacts were found in various levels from the subsurficial sheet trash levels to the bottoms of features. The flakes and points were primarily of basalt, rhyolite, chert, and jasper, and the ground stone artifacts were made from vesicular basalt or quartzite (Table 4.4).

Prehistoric Hohokam sherds were found only in feature 15 and 17. One of these small plainware fragments came from Feature 15 and two were found in Feature 17.

Given the quantity of lithic debris, it appears that an Archaic period site must have been located on Block 228. Possibly a small Hohokam site was located on this block as well. The sites from which the prehistoric artifacts were derived were destroyed sometime during the historic occupation of the block after about 1872.

Summary and Final Comments

The Tucson Convention Center Expansion Project studied 14 features within three lots, lots 6 and 17, which were related, and Lot 7. These features included privies, wells, large circular pits, and a number of less well defined trash pits and lenses, all containing various quantities of the debris resulting from everyday living. Three of the trash pits and lenses were not excavated.

Feature No.	Lithic flakes & chipping waste	Pinto Point	Reworked Archaic point	Mano	Metate	Misc. Ground Stone	Plainware Sherd	Totals
2	6			2				8
4	27			1				28
5	16							16
6	97			1	1			99
7	15							15
8						1		1
9	1							1
10	8		1					9
11	15			1				16
15	37	1		2			1	41
17	7						2	9
TOTALS	229	1	1	7	1	1	3	243

TABLE 4.4
Prehistoric Artifacts

The 14 features all yielded artifacts which were useful in helping us better understand how Tucsonans lived 90 years ago, at the turn-of-the century. At that time, Tucson was a small community with most of its residents living in small adobe houses, often built in rows in the Sonoran style, without indoor plumbing or electricity. They used outdoor privies, obtained their drinking water from wells located a few feet from these privies, and some baked their bread in outdoor ovens. Tucsonans survived in heat of summer without the benefit of evaporative coolers or air conditioning. If a homeowner was fortunate enough to have electricity, as some were, only electric fans were available to mitigate the enervating heat. Sleeping outdoors was a common practice during the summer months. Not surprisingly, most of Tucson's residents were perfectly happy with that way of life.

The benefits of the Tucson Convention Center Archaeological Project to the community are many, but most are intangible and long term in scope. The project provides another chapter in our understanding of the life styles of early Tucsonans and how these have changed over time. It is useful to be aware of how far Tucson has progressed in a short time and to remind us of the changes in our urban environment. Very little is known of the lives of the ordinary people in Tucson at the turn of the century and earlier. This is especially true of the minorities and the poor. In many cases, archaeology provides the only means and methods for acquiring information about these people.

Archaeologically interesting and informative artifacts and other data, that otherwise would have been destroyed, have been collected and will be preserved for others to see and study. The project will be of value for those performing future archaeological excavations in urban Tucson. The data in this report can be used for comparative purposes, and it provides one small slice of information from which the history of the ordinary citizen of Tucson will ultimately be written.

It is important to have an understanding of the past, if for no other reason than to help explain the present, but having an understanding of the past will not prevent us from repeating the mistakes of the past. Seven of the 14 features could be associated with two families, the Peter Bradys who lived on Lot 6 and the Charles Von Erxlebens who resided on Lot 7. The Bradys occupied their house for 14 years from 1899 to 1913 and the Von Erxlebens were on Lot 6 for 10 years from 1894 to 1904. Unfortunately those responsible for the trash deposits created before and after these two families could not be identified. The historical record simply was not complete enough to make those identifications.

There were a number of similarities and differences between the two families. They lived on Block 228 at the same time and undoubtedly knew each other. Both families owned their own homes which were constructed of adobe. This block was consistently residential in character throughout its history. The Von Erxleben home was larger and on a larger lot than was the Brady home. The former was on Main Street and the latter on Meyer Street. The Main Street side of the block appears to have been more affluent and more Anglo in population composition than the Meyer Street side, which was more traditional in appearance.

Peter Brady, a well known Arizona pioneer, was an Anglo with a Mexican born wife. His household of eight contained other Mexican born women who were relatives of his wife. Von Erxleben was born in Germany and his wife was from England. His household contained six people.

Both men were involved in one way or another with mining. Brady's occupation was "miner" and Von Erxleben was listed as both a civil and a mining engineer. At one time Von Erxleben was a U.S. Mineral Surveyor. The only evidence found relating to their mining related occupations were mineral specimens found in features in both lots. Brady features 2 and 9 contained what appeared to be copper ore specimens and Feature 4 on Lot 7 had copper and lead specimens. On the basis of occupation Von Erxleben would seem to have had a higher professional ranking than Brady, but Brady, as an early Arizona pioneer, was held in relatively high esteem.

On the basis of the artifacts, many similarities existed between the two families. Both households preferred the more expensive cuts of beef. The families also used similar ceramic types. Papago and Mexican pottery was used in both households for cooking and other purposes. The use of these ceramics for cooking purposes by the Von Erxleben family was unexpected as they were thought to have been used primarily within the Mexican community. Apparently, however, some Anglo families, possibly the less affluent ones, emulated the Mexican pattern in this regard.

Based upon their ethnic backgrounds and occupations, the residents of both lots, especially Von Erxleben, would have been expected to have been above average in economic status. The artifacts should have demonstrated this, yet the evidence suggests that both families were living relatively simple lives, not burdened with excess fancy foods, numerous alcoholic beverages, and the like. Based on the Mexican and Papago pottery, the plain hardpaste white earthenwares and porcelain, and food types, the living standards of the two families were not dissimilar. There is a suggestion in the use of the relatively inexpensive Mexican and Papago ceramics for cooking purposes and in the use of hardpaste white earthenwares, that perhaps Von Erxleben did not enjoy the economic status that his occupation would imply. It may be that Brady and Von Erxleben lived a very similar life style.

REFERENCES

Arizona Directory Co.
  1932   *Tucson City Directory, 1934.* Tucson: Arizona Directory Co.

  1934   *Tucson City Directory, 1934.* Tucson: Arizona Directory Co.

  1935   *Tucson City Directory, 1935.* Tucson: Arizona Directory Co.

Ayres, James E.
   1984   Rosemont: The History and Archaeology of post-1880 Sites in the Rosemont
Area,   Santa Rita Mountains, Arizona. *Arizona State Museum Archaeological
Series* 147(3).   Tucson: University of Arizona.

     1988a   Overview report for historic sites: Tucson Convention Center Expansion Project.
              MS on file, Cultural Resource Management Division, Arizona State Museum:
              University of Arizona: Tucson.

     1988b   Overview Report for Historic Sites: Tucson Convention Center Expansion
              Project. MS on file, Cultural Resource Management Division, Arizona State
              Museum, The University of Arizona.

Ayres, James E.
     1988c   Tucson Convention Center Expansion Project: Research Design. MS on file,
              Cultural Resource Management Division, Arizona State Museum, The University
              of Arizona.

Barnes, Frank C.
   1972   *Cartridges of the World.* Revised Fourth Edition. DBI Books, Inc. Northfield,
           IL.

Barter, G. W. (Compiler)
   1881   *Directory of the City of Tucson for the Year 1881.* San Francisco: H. S.
           Crocker & Co.

Devner, Kay
   1968   Patent Medicine Picture. Tombstone Epitaph, Tombstone, AZ.

Fike, Richard
   1987   *The Bottle Book. A Comprehensive Guide to Historic Embossed Medicine
           Bottles.* Salt Lake City: Gibbs M. Smith.

Flayderman, Norm
    1983   *Flayderman's Guide to Antique American Firearms ... and Their Values*. 3rd
            Edition. Northfield, IL: DBI Books.

Fontana, Bernard L.
    1968   Bottles and history: the case of Magdalena de Kino, Sonora. Mexico. *Historical
            Archaeology* 2:45-55.

Foundation, Brand Names
    1947   *43,000 Years of Public Service*. Brand Names Foundation, New York.

Gates, William C. , Jr. and Dana Ormerod
    1982   The East Liverpool pottery district: Identification of manufacturers and marks.
            <u>Historical Archaeology</u> 16 (1&2).

Giarde, Jeffrey L.
    1980   *Glass Milk Bottles: Their Makers and Marks*. Bryn Mawr, CA: Time Travelers
            Press.

Godden, Geoffrey A.
    1964   *Encyclopedia of British Pottery and Porcelain Marks*. New York: Bonanza
            Books.

Heerman Stationery, Co.
    1903   *Pima County, A. T. Directory, 1903-4*. Tucson: Heerman Stationery Co.

Henry, Susan L.
    1987   Factors influencing consumer behavior in turn-of-the-century Phoenix, Arizona.
            In *Consumer Choice in Historical Archaeology*, edited by Suzanne M. Spencer
            Wood. New York: Plenum Press.

Herskowitz, Robert M.
    1978   Fort Bowie Material Culture, *Anthropological Papers of the University of
            Arizona* 31. Tucson: University of Arizona Press.

Holscher, Harold H.
    1965   Hollow and specialty glass: background and challenge. *The Glass Industry* 46.
            Reprint. Toledo: Owens-Illinois.

Hull-Walski, Deborah A. and James E. Ayres
    1989   The Historical Archaeology of Dam Construction Camps in Central Arizona,
            Vol. 3, Laboratory Methods and Data Computerization. MS on file, Phoenix:
            Dames and Moore.

Israel, Fred L. (Editor)
    1968   *1897 Sears Roebuck Catalogue*. New York: Chelsea House Publishers.

Kendrick, Grace
    1963   *The Antique Bottle Collector*. Sparks, NV: Western Printing and Publishing Co.

Kimball, F.E.A. (Compiler)
    1908   *Tucson City Directory, 1908*. Tucson: F.E.A. Kimball.

Kovel, Ralph and Terry Kovel
    1986   *Kovel's New Dictionary of Marks*. New York: Crown Publishers.

Lehner, Lois
    1980   *Complete Book of American Kitchen and Dinner Wares*. Des Moines: Wallace - Homestead Book.

Logan, Herschel C.
    1959   *Cartridges: A Pictorial Digest of Small Arms Ammunition*. New York: Bonanza Books.

Periodical Publishers, Association
    1934   *Trade-Marks*. New York: Periodical Publishers Association.

Pritchett, Jack and Allen Pastron
    1983   Ceramic dolls as chronological indicators: implications from a San Francisco Dump Site. In "Forgotten Places and Things: Archaeological Perspectives on American History," compiled and edited by Albert E. Ward. *Contributions to Anthropological Studies* 3. Albuquerque: Center for Anthropological Studies.

Randall, Mark
    1971   Early Marbles. *Historical Archaeology* 1971: 102-105.

Sheridan, Thomas E.
    1986   *Los Tucsonense. The Mexican Community in Tucson, 1854-1941*. Tucson: The University of Arizona Press.

Skinner, A. P.
    1906   *Tucson City, Pima County and Santa Cruz County Directory, 1906-7*. Tucson: A.P. Skinner Co.

Stitt, Irene
    1974   *Japanese Ceramics of the Last 100 Years*. New York: Crown Publishers.

Toulouse, Julian H.
    1971   *Bottle Makers and Their Marks*. New York: Thomas Nelson.

Tucson City Directory, Co.

1908   *Directory of the City of Tucson and Pima County, Arizona, 1908.*   Tucson: Tucson City Directory, Co.

Tucson Directory , Co.
1917   *Tucson City Directory, 1918.*   Tucson: Tucson Directory Co.

1918   *Tucson City Directory, 1918.*   Tucson: Tucson Directory Co.

Wilson, William L. and Betty Wilson
1971   *19th Century Medicine in Glass.*   Eau Gallie, FL: 19th Century Hobby and Publishing.

Zumwalt, Betty
1980   *Ketchup, Pickles, Sauces - 19th Century Food in Glass.*   Fulton, CA: Mark West Publishers.